Crossing

the

Threshold

of Death

Roberto Saldivar

Preparation for publication: *www.specialnovels.com*
Author's e-mail: *saldivarmsps@aol.com*

First edition

Foreword

The path of God's mystery is manifested in our humanity and in every prayer, every rosary and every tender look we give to His face of light; asking... He returns it infinitely in perfect ways. Sometimes, we make that request to God by telling a loved one about Him and sometimes by showing that the impossible is possible in heaven as it is on earth.

Father Roberto expresses these infinite possibilities. I faithfully believe that, in complicity, God and he shared his tenderness with us through this miraculous manifestation of which we are witnesses.

Each experience shared through this book invites us to risk taking God's compass to confront ourselves and be grateful for His presence. It is an honor to have shared some tear-pearls for humanity. I hope that each person receives the message for which Father Roberto, a human being like you and me, is also responsible.

Enjoy and take what our Heavenly Father transmits to you through Father Roberto of his miracle made message to you reader.

María del Carmen Morga,
Psychotherapist

Index

Prologue

Our humanity causes the tension between our infinite desires and our limits to allow us to recognize our dependence on others and ultimately on God. In the awareness of our suffering, we become conscious of God's compassion and love for humankind. We can open or close our hearts to the possibility of allowing ourselves to be comforted and healed, even in the midst of pain, and when the probable outcome is not the desired one.

Suffering is inherently undesirable. We would like to prevent it or at least reduce it, but even if that were possible, at the end-of-life suffering is inevitable. Pain is an inseparable part of the mystery of our existence. In so many occasions when there is no escape, as has happened during the COVID-19 pandemic, we can ask ourselves: What does it mean to be rescued from illness, from suffering and even from death? Would a full life, in constant growth and with infinite perspectives, be possible without difficulties or risks? Would our aspirations be enough without having to suffer?

But in truth, only Jesus Christ can open and broaden the horizon of existence for us, filling us with a hope that is consolation, peace and joy. The mysteries of Christ's Incarnation, passion, death and Resurrection trace for us an ever-ascending path that crosses any barrier and takes advantage of them all. Because of the good news, which is Jesus himself, human suffering and even death find another full meaning, a fuller sense. The whole of life passes from mere monotonous passage to transcendence, despise suffering, and by means of it. This happens not despite suffering but because suffering is voluntarily united to the sacrifice of the Son of God on the Cross.

With his sacrifice on the Cross, Jesus has set the standard for us to give meaning to life and with it, to its decisive moments, such as the recovery and convalescence of Rev. Fr. Roberto Saldívar, MSpS. The Lord knows that we always need close examples that cause his teachings to be visible to us in explicit ways. In Father Saldívar, God grants us the testimony of a man, a priest of Christ, who at the most critical moment has known how to offer himself as a living victim. But beyond his own docile acceptance of the divine will, in Father Roberto himself, we have been blessed by verifying the gratuitous healing power of Jesus, doctor of bodies and souls.

As a testimony of grace, this book is not the narrative of a mere human going through a difficult time. It's not even just an inspiring and impressive story. The cry of joy of a heart burns because the Lord has passed and has touched his disciple, Fr. Roberto. He cannot stop proclaiming the wonders of his Lord who has saved him. Following the example of the Lord, who preserves the wounds of his passion and death, Father Saldívar has returned renewed from the brink of death, as the title says, *"Crossing the Threshold of Death."* He is filled with renewed passion to fulfill the missionary call, made to him by the Holy Spirit, to proclaim the risen Jesus.

Most Rev. Archbishop Gustavo García Siller, MSpS
Archbishop of San Antonio

Introduction

On the verge of death, they sent me to another hospital in a helicopter because they did not have the machines to save my life. I was in a critical and terrifying situation; they talked about disconnecting me to avoid further suffering. This whole situation happened by surprise... death was the only thing talked about; surviving was impossible. What to do? Nobody knew, but: 'He's going to die anyway,' was what my relatives heard from the doctors who treated me.

'Surviving is impossible, he will have to cross the threshold of death and if he lives, he will have to learn to swallow, speak, walk and learn to be a priest,' these were the medical predictions. Four months later, I left the hospital in a wheelchair because my muscles weren't responding. I learned to eat, speak, walk and to celebrate mass because I am a priest of 'Christ', and I am also a 'Missionary of the Holy Spirit'. Prayers came like an electric shock, a lot of energy.

Illness is a mystery, and it usually surprises us, but it doesn't have to be always like this. What is certain is that we all suffer, and we each suffer differently. But fortunately, suffering can also be a grace; unfortunately, not everyone knows it. It is enough to read in the news to realize that many people suffer and/or are in terrible conditions. The question I now ask you is, how do you suffer? Do you know that your suffering can lessen if you accept it? But you have to learn how.

On September 5, 2020, I contracted COVID-19, was admitted to the hospital on September 8, and was hospitalized until November 19 of the same year. These months were difficult; I got worse day by day... This disease was difficult for the people around me, especially for my Community and my family. The prognoses they received from the doctors were dire; there was no hope of life; I was destined to die. My brain was dead, I was in a vegetative state. The doctors' recommendation was to disconnect me from the machines. Only a miracle could save me.

My family, my Community, members of the Church and friends, who were aware of my situation, knew that only a miracle could save me. So, they set out to pray continually for a miracle.

This book is my testimony of the miracle that God did in my life. I ask God that reading these pages helps you meditate on your life. I dedicated this book to my nephew (godson) Ricardo García, who lost his life to cancer on June 14, 2021; funeral that I celebrated being already, in clear recovery. I believe and hope this book can help you value the gift of life and undertake it with enthusiasm and gratitude, having gone through this trance led me to reflect that life goes by quickly. The real and amazing miracle I received is that I am still living. God, who defeated death, gave me the privilege of continuing on this earth. God is always present, and he is even more so when we suffer in any way and when we fight for a better world. Isn't this the purpose of our existence? Isn't this what keeps us in God?

In this book, I will share my experience, hoping it will help you to meditate on your own salvation story. In the first chapter, I will share *"To Live in God"* (when we live for God, we die to everything around us). The second chapter is titled *"Towards Recovery"* I will share what my recovery involved, the fragility of life and what the disease entails from my own experience. The next chapter is *"Vulnerability"*, where I openly share my experience and how it transformed me... living again made me more aware of human vulnerability, that was an important gift from God. I have dedicated a chapter to *"Father Félix de Jesús Rougier."* I attribute the miracle of my healing to this holy man who dearly loved Jesus and Mary. His reference to Mary was, "With Mary Everything, without Her Nothing." Father Félix was the founder of our Congregation of Missionaries of the Holy Spirit and he is special to all of us. In the next chapter, I will share *"Hope and Suffering."* When I speak of hope, I think of a phrase I learned from writer William Faulkner, *"You cannot swim into new seas until you have lost your fear and trust that you no longer have to see the water's edge."* I have added a special chapter, *"Finding Calm through Meditation."* I liked this chapter because in it, I share seven meditations that will help you in this time we are living. My family has been praying the rosary since before I got sick, and what better way to include a chapter with the name, *"Holy Mary Mother of God."* The last chapter, *"God wants us Healthy,"* I share the importance of health... If God wants us healthy, you must believe it. In this chapter, I will prove it to you with 50 biblical quotes, I think they help you.

Finally, I invite you to believe in God and believe in miracles. I am a faithful testimony that miracles exist. Remember that we are alive and

God is with us, always... you and I are true miracles, **true miracles**!

To Live in God

I would like to begin this book with a prayer from Saint Augustine because it sums up well my feeling of gratitude to God:

Lord Jesus, let me know myself and know You,
And desire nothing but only You.
Let me hate myself and love You.
Let me do everything for the sake of You.
Let me humble myself and exalt You.
Let me think of nothing except You.
Let me die to myself and live in You.
Let me accept whatever happens as from You.
Let me banish myself and follow You,
And ever desire to follow You.
Let me fly from myself and take refuge in You,
That I may deserve to be defended by You.
Let me fear for myself, let me fear You,
Let me be among those who are chosen by You.
Let me distrust myself and put my trust in You.
Let me be willing to obey for the sake of You.
Let me cling to nothing save only to You,

Let me be poor because of You.
Look upon me, that I may love You.
Call me that I may see You,
And forever enjoy You."[1]

Throughout my life, I do not remember having suffered, I cannot remember any painful experience, but I have known people who suffer, and I have seen the suffering of my loved ones. Nobody wants to suffer, but we all suffer in one way or another. What is true is that we all want to be happy. We talk about many things, but rarely about happiness and health, even though happiness depends largely on health, they produce a unique energy, they drive and stimulate us, they lead us to a feeling of freedom, even while suffering. Happiness should always be our goal. We must be happy and take delight in life. Isn't happiness what God wants for each one of us? Life is oriented to it, but this is only achieved when we experience love, especially when we have someone special to love. This pandemic is leading us to value life and love.

Unfortunately, over 5 million people have died worldwide because of the COVID Virus (COVID-19). Life changed for all. I have written this book to share my story and the miracle that God did in me through the intercession of Father Félix de Jesús Rougier.

As I look back at the experiences I have lived, I can honestly say that everything I have, everything that has illuminated my existence has

---

1   *Confessions. San Agustin. New York City Press, Introduction and traduced by María Boulding O.S.B. Hyde Park New York. 1997 (Translated from the Spanish).*

been knowing the Spirituality of the Cross that intensified thanks to this COVID experience. The cross brought me closer to Christ.

What better time to follow Jesus our savior than today? Now the question --- Do you believe in Jesus? And who is Jesus to you? Do you live conquered by Jesus?

If Jesus has won you over then you have his love and vitality, you are inflamed with joy and everything you do gives heat, it inflames. Love and joy have something in common: both open the heart and both widen it.

Whoever can be entirely in the present leaves the cycle of time for an instant and feels immobile time --- eternity, and that is when we enter the cycle of love. That is why I could say to the person I love: you will not die. Love survives time; it is fullness. That is why the hours that count are the hours not counted. Whoever counts the hours does not live in the present time. To better understand time, we must understand what it is, to belong and to be part of the other. To love is to enter the integral path of life, living with an open heart in the present time, where my brother is not a stranger but part of my life. When we come into contact with the heart, the integral part of love, we enter the love that is relationship. This is the consciousness that the human needs to integrate love and open up to life. We need to love to live in the present.

Love is energy that comes from God; that is why He is the Alpha and the Omega (cf. Revelation 21, 6). The mystery of God as a person is because God is communion. In communion, God is perfect. Love is only given in communion with God[2]. God is love, and love is the dominant quality of God and the most attractive. God's love is infinite; his love emanates unity and is the beginning of the same unity from which everything begins, the source of life. Every created being of all time had its beginning in God, whose depth exceeds all knowledge.

We hope to achieve the divinity of God's fruitful love. Every created being is a breath of divine love and proceeds from God from all eternity to life. The singer Joy Williams expresses beautifully in her song "*When Creation was Young*." I invite you to take some time to listen to it and meditate on your own existence in this world, you are created in the image and likeness of God --- you are created out of love to commune with God in love:

When Creation was young
Before rivers learned to run
Before hell caught fire
And God made the sun
When Creation was young
Before Adam fell for Eve
Before birds found melody
Before the apple hit the ground not far from the tree
Before Adam fell for Eve

---

2   *Have you ever wondered why when we receive the Eucharist, we call it Communion? The answer is simple, we receive the body of Christ and in Him we unite. Communion is the union between the words common and union.*

11

Oh, I was loving you
I was loving you
I was loving you
Loving you
Before gold found the hills
Before field felt a blade of a till
Before the sky was black as coal and the Earth stood still
Before gold found the hills
Oh, I was loving you
I was loving you
I was loving you
Loving you
Before you, you took a breath
Before sin ever confessed
Before hate was a word and life found death
Before you, you took a breath
Oh, I was loving you
I was loving you
I was loving you
Loving you
When creation was young
Before rivers learned to run
Before hell caught fire and God made the sun
When creation was young

God loves us and, therefore, we will suffer less. If we cry when we suffer, our tears will be precious, like little pearls. These tears will have the strength to dignify us, make us holy, they will reward what is broken in the heart. Let us sanctify our tears, so we can raise them above the superfluous world. Then in the midst of them we can give glory to God and to all creation.

When we sanctify our tears, we sanctify suffering, which is transitory. Suffering helps us appreciate the beauty of life and to realize what we must correct or improve in our relationship with others. This is a lifelong task, yes, but it produces a life that becomes calmer, kinder, and more fulfilling. When we accept and value suffering, we will discover its vitality, and thus we can suffer properly. Suffering should not be an obstacle to happiness, and when we understand its value, it is never an obstacle. We suffer for the love of Christ and in union with him. Suffering should not lead to depression either. Effective suffering is that which is united to Christ, where the mystery of the Cross is experienced. Like the olive tree and the vine, which live on almost no water, they still grow and bear much fruit. So also, with suffering, we grow and bear fruit. The Lord, in his love, will allow us to experience suffering and offer it for the good of others and for ourselves and thus we can say: **JESUS SAVIOUR OF MANKIND, SAVE THEM.** The implications of this prayer are far-reaching and will be effective. Many times, I have said this prayer, which was said first by Concepción Cabrera de Armida (Conchita). With the healing power of the cross, we recognize the wounds of the world, and we keep those wounds in the heart of Christ where the life of all is included (cf. Job 12, 10). Concepción Cabrera asked Jesus for this love and shares this beautiful thought with us:

13

During the final days of his life, Jesus, our model and teacher of all the virtues, spoke only about love. He asked for love from him who is Love itself, from the Person who is Love, and he promised the gift of the Spirit of Love. This Jesus, who is God and man, gives us the Holy Spirit; as man, this is his prayer for us, and as the God that he is, he gives him to us. Later, we will hear him say to the apostles, receive the Holy Spirit.[3]

Our gift to God is to offer the suffering of our heart. This will be the best thing we can do for our salvation. But this requires compassion and solidarity.[4] Compassion because with suffering, we stand in solidarity with all those who suffer, and solidarity because we unite with the one who suffers. Compassion and solidarity ask us to go where it hurts, to enter a place of suffering, to share the brokenness, fear, confusion and anguish of others. These two: compassion/solidarity --- challenges us to suffer with those who suffer, cry with those who cry. Be weak with those who are weak and vulnerable with those who are vulnerable. Suffering has a tender side, it is love, so it is important to learn to suffer, there we

---

3   *Cabrera de Armida, Concepcion, 'What Jesus Is Like,' Most Rev. Donald W. Montrose, Tr. 2008, The Fathers and Brothers of the Society of St. Paul, ST PAULS/Alba House, Staten Island, NY.*

4   *The word compassion is derived from the Latin words pati and cum, which together mean "to suffer with." The word solidarity comes also from the Latin solidus which means "firm, whole, undivided, trustworthy, genuine."*

unite with those who suffer. The singer Fito Páez expresses[5] it well in his song, 'Today I come to offer my heart.'

Who said everything is lost?
I come to offer my heart
So much blood that the river took
I come to offer my heart
It won't be that easy, but I know it will pass
It won't be as simple as I thought
How to open the chest and take out the soul
a slash of love
Moon of the poor, always open
I come to offer my heart
Like an unalterable document
I come to offer my heart
And I will unite the ends of the same bow
And I'll go easy, I'll go slowly
And I'll give you everything and you'll give me something
Something to ease me a little more
When no one is near or far
I come to offer my heart
When the satellites don't reach
I come to offer my heart

_____

5   *Argentine musician Fito Páez, 'Today I Come to Offer My Heart (Hoy Vengo a Ofrecer mi Corazón), 1985.*

And I speak of countries and hopes
I speak for life, I speak for nothing
I speak for changing this, our house
To change it just to change

Whoever wants to free himself from suffering must free himself from love, because there is no love without suffering, love always demands an element of sacrifice and pain. When we know this is what love demands, to come out of oneself, then we become human. We also understand that suffering is the process through which we mature and become more understanding and caring. That's why Fito Páez begins his song by asking, 'Who said that everything is lost?' Whoever consistently avoids suffering will not be able to truly love; he will become harsh and selfish.

If we live with compassion and solidarity, nothing will be lost. It will not be simple or easy, but in the heart of the Cross of the Apostolate, mercy will triumph and the world will then change. Until the heart truly "falls in love," we cannot be content with shallow prayer. Mario Benedetti (1920-2009) tells us in two beautiful sentences:

Love is not repetition.
Each act of love is a cycle in itself,
a closed orbit in its own ritual.

If the heart gets bored of loving, what good is it for?

Offering suffering is living life with courage and for this we need to be sensitive to all injustice. Justice is a Latin word that comes from the verb "divide" and divide can also mean "separate." We need to separate ourselves from sin so as not to divide ourselves internally. There is a saying that goes, "The unjust divides and separates." To this, I must also say that the person who lives justly will always join others. Why? Because such a person is always happy and will always share their happiness to others. Love must materialize into action; action is the most perfect expression of love and here there is always unity. You cannot do good by willing good to others; it must come with action (see Matthew 25:35-40). [6] This is what true spirituality consists of --- that which is realized with action.

Mahatma Gandhi used to say, "Think of the poorest person you have ever encountered and ask yourself if your next action will be to help him/her."[7] God challenges us to action. To understand the call to service, let us remember the invitation that Saint Teresa of Ávila calls us to:

> "Christ has no body now but yours. No hands, no feet
> on earth but yours. Yours are the eyes through which he
> looks with compassion on this world. Yours are the feet
> with which he walks to do good. Yours are the hands
> through which he blesses all the world. Yours are the
> hands, yours are the feet, yours are the eyes, you are his

---

6   *I was hungry, thirsty, naked, sick, a stranger and you 'GAVE ME...'*

7   *Guha, Ramachandra. Gandhi, The Years that Changed the World 1914-1948. Alfred A. Knopf. New York, 2018.*

body. Christ has no body now on earth but yours."[8]

We all have gifts and charisms that must be used for the good of all. Sad who does not recognize their gifts. This happens because charisms are unknown. Using our gifts to benefit others creates happiness, while not doing so leads to sadness. COVID, which I haven't come to understand yet, left me with tastes I didn't have before --- now I'm drinking sugary drinks, I like to serve, cook and play etc... it made me more aware of my surroundings. 'You have changed a lot,' my family tells me.

Being happy should be our mission. Did you know that pursuing happiness is one of the root causes of unhappiness? Many think that they can be happy by wishing for it. However, happiness cannot be found anywhere, it can be found only within oneself. To be happy you must be attentive to your interior and discover the richness of happiness in your heart. Happiness is in us because God left it there when he created us. Happiness does not come from things or through people. In this world, many are sad and the reasons are poverty, injustice, inequality, diseases and the current pandemic (COVID-19), among other things.

A little over two years ago, my sister came to tell me that her son had cancer.[9] With tears, she asked me to pray for him. I told her to trust God. One Sunday, sometime later, I was celebrating Mass and my sister was present. Curiously something strange happened, I turned my gaze to an

---

8   Negro Garcia, Marta Paula, Sch.: *Praying Without Protocols, A Search Made Encounter, Rodes Printing Miami, Florida, 2017. (Translate from Spanish)*

9   *At the end I have written about my godson and nephew Ricardo García-Saldívar, because I have dedicated this book to him.*

image of Blessed Concepción Cabrera de Armida located to my left, I felt at that moment she told me, 'Everything will be fine.' After Mass, I shared with my sister what I thought Conchita had told me. My sister was glad to hear what I shared and later confirmed that what I said helped her not to lose hope.

Death and the experiences of it are inevitable, I experienced the death of my parents. The passing of my mother (July 17, 2019) hurt the most. With her death, I felt that something of me died too. Death will leave us with a void that will be difficult to fill, and it contains a mystery difficult to understand. It can make us suffer more when it takes away those we love but let us remember that in suffering there can be peace and peace makes us reconcile with death. When my mother died, I felt she took something of me with her, my joys and my sufferings.

Death is inevitable, so we should reflect on how we would like to live the rest of the time we have left in this world. What will be our contribution, or what gift will we leave behind when we die? What would you like the epitaph on your grave to say? On my mother's grave it says a phrase of Saint Elizabeth Ann Seton, "God is mine and I am His."[10] We chose this saying because in recent years, my mother had great devotion to St. Elizabeth Ann Seton, and those were the words of Saint Elizabeth when she received her First Holy Communion.

Saying goodbye to my mother was difficult. It's difficult to say goodbye to the people we love; it is and will always be painful. Hence the importance we understand and accept the numerous life departures due

---

10   *Seton, Elizabeth Bayley. Collected Writings: Volume 1. New City Press, Hyde Park, New York. 2000.*

to death. The death of our loved ones prepares us to face the reality of our death, which is imminent.

When my mom died, I had the opportunity to say goodbye and apologize for the times I disobeyed her. I am grateful for the gift of my mom and dad, for the love they instilled in me to love God and those who have surrounded me throughout my life. My father Mateo died on March 14, 1990 --- it was also difficult.

Life and death are of paramount importance.
Time passes quickly and opportunities are lost.
Let's wake up! Awake!
Do not waste your life.[11]

What is generally known as "life" or "living" is full of uncertainty, death, is perhaps the most significant of all events in this life. For the vast majority, death is terrifying. Births are more beautiful. When a baby is born, we celebrate it with a party and congratulate the parents. There is an entire industry dedicated to celebrating birthdays: cake, parties, gifts, cards, etc. So why can't death also be next to life if one leads us to the other? William Shakespeare said that "to cry is to make mourning less deep". So not crying should lead us to celebrate better there are cultures that celebrate death with a party, and it includes cake and gifts, shouldn't we do the same?

Those who do not love themselves seldom love life. When pain

---

11   *Chernikoff, David. Life, Part Two. Seven Keys to awakening with purpose and joy as you age. Shambhala Publications, Inc, 2021.*

is avoided and relief is sought in material things, we end up isolated. Suffering can point the way to a greater wholeness of life and become a powerful force for healing. But if we live lovingly, this will help us to be prepared for the time of death, when God needs us home. God wants us to open ourselves to a broader vision of life, to stop resisting what we cannot change and to receive this life as a gift. Even when love doesn't eliminate suffering, God is always there for us. We always find a close God who encourages us, guiding us with love. No matter how much we may have suffered, the divine light within eases the pain. It is in tune with our experience of pain and leads us to God, giving us the confidence to be grateful for life and become aware of all that it has given us. I propose that you love to be fully happy.

Saint Teresa of Ávila spoke of life and how short it can be, she recommends:

"All life is short, and the life of some extremely short. And how do we know if ours won't be so short at the very hour or moment we determine to serve God completely it will come to an end? This is possible. In sum, there is no reason to give importance to anything that will come to an end. And who will not work hard if he thinks that each hour is the last? Well, believe me, thinking this is the safest course."[12]

---

12   Teresa of Avila, *The Way of Perfection, The Collected Works of Teresa of Avila,* trans. Kieran Kavanaugh and Otilio Rodriguez, chap. 3, no. 6., Washington, D.C: ICS Publications, 1987.

Some people intuitively know that their lives are ending. However young and healthy they may be and however illogical it may seem, they feel that death is near. Others know they will die because they have been diagnosed with an incurable and terminal illness. They live each suffering with hope, intensifying their relationship with God in a spiritual life that leads them to live more fully, enjoying the company of those around them, thus improving their quality of life, the little they have left. E. M. Forster wisely said: "Death destroys a man: the idea of death saves him."[13]

When they ask me if there is life after death, I usually answer they shouldn't worry about it, rather they should worry about living in the present moment, that they enjoy life now. You shouldn't worry because you know there is and you're preparing? It is not like this?

Most people fear death. This fear comes from the experience of not having lived long enough and wanting to continue living to enjoy the time we have left in our lives. I had to face death when I was infected with COVID. I was not afraid of death because I had lived a significant life as a priest. It was just hard to let 'go' and trust in God's will for me. Once the mystery of death is understood deep within one's being, you are not afraid of it. But there is an existential terror of losing the possibilities that lie ahead --- what you have never found. Something in me says --- 'I have not done it yet; I have not lived long enough. I have not touched the real, the good, the true and the beautiful, for which I was created.' When we

---

13   *Edward Morgan Forster was an English fiction writer, essayist and librettist. Many of his novels examine class difference and hypocrisy, including A Room with a View, Howards End and A Passage to India. These last brought him his greatest success which I invite read or see.*

have experienced life, we will reach the deathbed and like Saint Francis of Assisi we will say to death...

Welcome, sister death.
I am not afraid to let life go,
because I have life.
I am life. [14]

Death is the last threshold we all face. This is what Paul means when he says, "... to know him and the power of his resurrection and [the] sharing of his sufferings by being conformed to his death" (Philippians 3,10).

Suffering makes us aware of death. It gives us hope because we know that after having suffered, we will live a full life. We die to be born in God who is love itself. Every miracle is proof of love; illness and suffering can be a miracle, even death itself brings us to the final miracle of eternal life --- life with God, the life of light. Following Christ is committing ourselves to being Christ's light and presence for others. This glorious world is within our reach if we awaken to the power of inner love, which creates the light of Christ.

Preparing ourselves for death makes us live the present fully. We think that we will have time when the years go by. However, we first must know what this time will entail. Life is short and God will call us to an account sooner rather than later. This is what Rosario Castellanos says in one of

---

14   Chesterton, Gilbert Keith. *CreateSpace Independent Publishing Platform, 2014.*

her many poems:

Behold, death takes as long as oblivion.
It is slowly invading us, pore by pore.
It is useless to run, rush,
always fleeing inventive new paths
and it is also useless to be still
without even breathing so that it doesn't hear us.

Every minute is an arrow in vain
fired at her
effective in turning against us.
Useless to be stunned and have for a celebration
because when we return, inevitably,
late at night, when you open the door ajar
we will find her motionless waiting for us.
And we can't escape living
because Life is one of those masks.
And nothing protects us from its fury
nor submissive humility towards her whip
nor the violent delivery
to the closed circle of her arms.[15]

When we have finished our life for this world, God will be there. God is eternal and his dynamism of love will expand in us in a process of

---

15   Castellanos, Rosario. *Poesía No Eres Tú. Obra Poética (1948-1971). Excerpt from 'Trayectoria del Polvo' pg. 26. Fondo de Cultural Económica. 1975: Ciudad de México (Translated from the Spanish) 26.*

new creation. This is love that generates and longs to be visible in the blossoming of our life. God wants to be born in us and for that we must die. This is what Saint Paul tells the Romans when he speaks of putting off the old man to the new man/woman (see Romans 6, 6). This is how Ralph Martin expresses it in his book "The Fulfillment of all Desire":

> *The whole purpose of our creation, the whole purpose of our redemption is so that we may be fully united with God in every aspect of our being. We exist for union; we were created for union; we were redeemed for eternal union. The sooner we're transformed the happier and more "fulfilled" we'll be. The only way to the fulfillment of all desire is to undertake and complete the journey to God.[16]*

Saint Paul also speaks of death when he writes his letter to the Corinthians --- "Where is your victory, oh death? Where, oh grave, your sting? The sting of death is sin, and the power of sin is the law; but thanks be to God, who gives us the victory through our Lord Jesus Christ" (1 Corinthians 15, 55-57). Death is the path to a new life. Even in death, everything is becoming something new. Therefore, death seems final only until we realize that it is the only way we can be born into new life. It is impossible that we know what all this means yet, but what we know is that one day we will die, hence the importance to love every single moment.

---

16   Martin, Ralph "The Fulfillment of all Desire," Emmaus Road Publishing. Steubenville, Ohio. 2006.

Love must be embodied in physical reality to be itself. God loves us and teaches us to love, that's why God "needs" us and we need him too. The way to God is Jesus.

Every moment of our lives involves a small death, life itself gives us opportunities to glimpse death. But the sad thing is that most people are usually distracted and few take full advantage of these opportunities. However, there is a way to relate to the small deaths of each day that will help you prepare for your own death. You have to realize that there is a death in every moment, in every relationship that ends… a flower that withers, food spoils, or things that no longer work. These deaths we experience throughout the days, ironically bring more positive than negative. Still, we make a big deal out of every death we experience, labeling it "negative."

Jesus said: "I am the way the truth and **the life**. No one comes to the Father except through me" (John 14, 6). He came to promise us that this mystery called life is eternal, but will we know how to enter it now? Will that path be ours?

For this God was radically involved in the world to be with us (Immanuel). It is in this regard that Dietrich Bonhoeffer says: "When Jesus crucified is called the image of the invisible God, the meaning is that this is God, and God is this way. --- to be with us."[17]   It is in the throbbing of the crucifixion that God reveals his love to us. Christ is really on the cross, dead from excess of love. But this Christ is God, and God is

---

17   *Metaxas, Eric, "Dietrich Bonhoeffer, The Cost of Discipleship. Simon and Schuster, New York*

like this, repeating what Bonhoeffer says, God has died to save humanity locked up in sin and there to make the true light shine, there the Christian can ascend to the light of Christ, the true light, the only one that shines in the darkness. The Cross of Christ is truly a threshold, a victory, with Christ the impossible is possible.

The Cross has approached me and invites me to abandon myself in it. Love can only reach its peak if it dominates suffering. Love is salvation and there detachment is defined. Jesus abandons himself to the Father, so we hear from him when he is in the garden of olive trees, *'Father, if you want, take this cup away from me; but not my will, but yours be done.'* His abandonment was total openness to God. Is abandonment for you an opening to light and life? Teilhard de Chardin explains what this detachment means:

> *Indeed, the living logic of action is that we could not conquer or enlarge ourselves except by dying little by little to ourselves. To act worthily, usefully... is to unite. But to join is to become someone greater than oneself.*[18]

Sad that we have pushed him out of us by our sins to the cross. He is weak and powerless in the world, and that is precisely the way, the only way, that He is to help and support us. The letter to the Hebrews (12, 1-2) invites us to fix our eyes on Jesus so He can help us leave sin:

---

18   Dupleix, Andre. *Orar con Pierre Teilhard de Chardin (Praying with Pierre Teilhard de Chardin)*. Sal Terrae, Santander, 2013 pg.48, *(translated from the English).*

Therefore, since we are surrounded by so great a cloud of witnesses, let us rid ourselves of every burden and sin that clings to us and persevere in running the race that lies before us while keeping our eyes fixed on Jesus, the leader and perfecter of faith. For the sake of the joy that lay before him he endured the cross, despising its shame, and has taken his seat at the right of the throne of God.

The Bible speaks of suffering through the martyrdom of Jesus; God helps humanity and all creation that groans with labor pains (see Romans 8:22).[19] That is why to believe in the unconditional love of God is to enter into his intimacy and suffering. Sadly, we forget God today even as we see Jesus as he was immersed in a culture of violence and conflict in the past. But Christ also knew the deepest truth hidden beneath the surface of human judgment. Therefore, we cannot be distressed and broken. We must ask God for faith and believe that His Kingdom is among us. Faith is more than a magic formula to overcome the worry, regret, shame, and resentment that clouds our vision. Having faith does not eliminate doubt or the weaknesses of our human condition. Faith is what leads us to the deepest truth that says that we are spiritual beings and the image of unlimited and unimaginable love.

The illness allowed me to further deepen my faith. It was an

---

19   *Roman 8:22-23: We know that all creation is groaning in labor pains even until now; and not only that, but we ourselves, who have the first fruits of the Spirit, we also groan within ourselves as we wait for adoption, the redemption of our bodies.*

experience I felt like a fire in my heart that led me to surrender my ego, and not have control in my hands, but in the hands of the doctors, nurses… letting God guide me. Priest Richard Rohr puts it this way:

> *This is probably why Jesus praised faith and trust even more than love. It takes a foundational trust to fall or to fail—and not to fall apart. Faith alone holds you while you stand waiting and hoping and trusting. Then, and only then, will deeper love happen. It's no surprise at all that in English (and, I am told, in other languages as well) we speak of "falling" in love. I think falling is the only way to get to authentic love. None would go freely, if we knew ahead of time what love is going to ask of us. Very human faith lays the necessary foundation for the ongoing discovery of love. Have no doubt, though: great love is always a discovery, a revelation, a wonderful surprise, a falling into "something" much bigger and deeper that is literally beyond us and larger than us.*[20]

Through faith, we can risk loving, falling in love, even though rejected and persecuted. God risks loving us because his love carries the possibility of being rejected. God's love respects our independence and our freedom

---

20   Rohr, Richard, *The Naked Now (Learning to See as the Mystics See)*, - *El Desnudo Ahora (Aprendiendo a Ver como Ven los Místicos)* - The Crossroad Publishing Company, New York, 2019.

because God does not seek to control, dominate or manipulate us. Rather, his love seeks to empower us and to cause us to flourish. God is not deaf to the cries of the poor or the suffering. Jesus Christ, who is God, is not deaf or indifferent to pain. He participates in the suffering we humans experience to elevate us to the glory of the deepest love. We become transformed as we unite our sufferings with Christ's intense sufferings on the cross. Jesus bears witness to the fidelity of divine love to transform us to a new life. His divine crucifixion revealed unconditional love, because there God himself fell in love to reveal and lead us to Divine love.

In God's humility, in his condescension, he came to live among us as a weak human with no prestige or power. He lived simply with few material amenities such that he was rejected by many. How could this be the long-awaited savior of humankind? The cross reveals God's heart to us because it reveals the vulnerability of God's love. It is the exit of God toward danger and nothingness; therefore, his fundamental disposition to reach the end of love, his cruel death on the cross.

The mystery of the cross is the mystery of God. It is a God who is not possessive and who fully communicates the mystery of love in a radical openness and acceptance of the human person. Love is in the person, not in the idea. Love is not a concept, but a powerful transforming energy that heals, reconciles, unites, and is the beginning of creation. Love is the divinity of God. That is why the cross is significant, not as an object of devotion, but because it gives us a God who reveals love. No one and nothing can undermine the humble person's trust in God. Once we get to know God as a God of love, nothing can dissuade us from committing ourselves to his will. Nothing can convince us to adapt to a world whose greed is overwhelming and whose arrogance is suffocating.

Then we will seek to know ourselves well and this can be achieved only by knowing God first. Saint John of the Cross invites us to this and says this is the fundamental thing in the spiritual life: "While we are in this earth nothing is more important to us than humility... In my opinion we shall never completely know ourselves if we don't strive to know God. By gazing at His grandeur, we get in touch with our own lowliness; by looking at His purity, we shall see our own filth; by pondering His humility, we shall see how far we are from being humble."[21]

In Latin, humility means earth. Only those who are humble recognize their condition as part of the earth because we were created from it (cf. Genesis 2, 7). Even if we have all the virtues, if we lack humility, we are imperfect. And it is easy to be humble because if we think about it with fairness, it is not a feat to be who we are. Only those with the courage to see their own humanity and their limitations can be humble like Mary. Whoever hides behind falsehood will not have the strength to resist sin. Those who are humble recognize their own truth which helps them to recognize their own limitations and deficiencies --- even when that is painful for them; because it has turned them into fertile land.

Humility is the precondition for having a true and authentic experience with God. We come to him in our nothingness with total trust, and we know he is always listening to us and loving us. That is the reason it is important to pray for each other --- by helping each other

---

21   *John of the Cross, The Spiritual Canticle, The Collected Works of St. John of the Cross, trans. Kieran Kavanaugh, OCD, Otilio Rodriguez, OCD, (Washington, D.C.: ICS Publications, 1991).*

deal with whatever pain and suffering we may face. Only then can we be truly humble when we recognize our interrelatedness with others and with creation (with all cosmic life). This is where we can say we have 'our feet on the ground' --- remember the definition of humility.

Thinking about the earth, much of it is unstable and fragile; when Jesus Crucified is called "the image of the invisible God", the meaning is this is God, and God is like that. God is not more glorious than in his humiliation. God is no more glorious than he is in his self-giving. God is not more powerful than in his impotence.[22] God is no more divine than he is in his humanity. All that can be said of God is on the cross. With outstretched arms, the crucified Christ embraces the sinful world turned upside down by human violence, disconnected and incomplete. A God radically in love with the world. The power of divine love is revealed in the cross as I mentioned before quoting Dietrich Bonhoeffer.

On the cross, the Incarnation of Christ achieves its true meaning and purpose. Therefore, the whole event of Christ must be understood in relation to the cross. There the self-sacrificing love of God is incarnated with extreme radicality. He gave himself as an oblation in renunciation and self-abandonment and revealed his divine love for us humans. That is why the cross means that God is deeply involved with the world. We suffer because we are personally vulnerable; we can lose our health, our family, our friends, our job, and everything that is precious to us. This suffering can be called suffering as deprivation. However, we can also

---

22   Metaxas, Eric, "Dietrich Bonhoeffer, *The Cost of Discipleship. Simon and Schuster, New York.*

suffer because our friends or family are vulnerable; our hearts are torn because they have lost something that is precious to them. We suffer with them because we identify with them.

In his Divine fullness, God loves those who suffer his pains, and carries his burdens with him. The love of God is the power of love to heal and transform death into life, that is why God is more divine in suffering. Therefore, the cross stands as the center; here we see what God is in the scandalous death of Jesus. Love shows us the power of embracing death and leads us to the fullness of life. The cross is the symbol of the fidelity of God's love for us and for creation. Whoever knows and lives the Spirituality of the Cross (which was inspired by Blessed Concepción Cabrera de Armida) will know what this secret contains.

In the crucifixion, God is light to the world, thus giving birth to our light. In life something always dies, and something is born --- The divine love of God lived by Jesus on the cross gives us hope of new life in the light. Loving now means letting God enter our hearts even in any illness or problems and transforming love into an offering. The crucifixion is the beginning of a new life. It is not a whisper lost in the wind; it is a cry heard above the storms of life. The crucifixion has brought us abundant life and now God invites us to be disciples of Christ with our offered sacrifice and suffering we participate in salvation; we are disciples of the crucified.

The crucifixion is the great divine "Yes." God through the death and sacrifice of his Son gives us life in abundance. All creation is under the aura of the cross, history, with its violence and atrocities, natural disasters and diseases, including every type of "pandemic", everything is protected by the cross --- there is the Son of God, there God will always be. We must trust him, be willing to participate in his creation, which he entrusted to us for his care.

The heart of God burns in each of us when we unite with Him, who dwells in the depths of our hearts. But if we only focus on protecting our heart, we can avoid a lot of pain, and we would live only half of life. Saint Therese of Lisieux shared his love, in her book 'Story of a Soul' she describes this beautifully:

> When the human heart gives itself to God, it loses nothing of its innate tenderness; in fact, this tenderness grows when it becomes more pure and more divine.[23]

Personally, for me, after the bitter experience of not having brain activity, cardiac activity, nor respiratory activity (practically dead), I gave my heart to God, I abandoned myself to Him and it is the fruit of the miracle that God did in me through the intercession of Father Félix de Jesús Rougier I can say that God exists, that God is alive. All hope was gone when the doctor told my family I needed to be taken off ECMO, ventilator and all other machines. All my family were worried and they continued to pray for a miracle for God to bring me back to life as all my organs had failed, and that is what happened. God gave me one more chance. It was a true miracle, and miracles like this are also within your

---

23   Therese of Lisieux, *Story of a Soul*, trans. John Clarke, OCD, Washington, DC: ICS Publications, 1996. chap. 1, p. 34.

reach if you really trust God and ask for it.

When we have experienced a cross of great suffering, we know that we can receive more crosses and help others face their crosses. The hope that we will bring to them will become the only sure gift that will give them joy to accept the pain that suffering brought them. Suffering is what makes us kind and compassionate towards them. So, having survived the first injustice, the first loss---suffering will bring more hope and security in pain. This experience has strengthened me and made me more sensitive, and empathetic to the suffering and pain of others, I cannot be indifferent to human pain, less to the injustices that cause suffering to the most vulnerable.

On November 29, 2019, Pope Francis said, "The Lord tells us to be prepared for the encounter, death is an encounter; it is He who comes to meet us. it is He who comes to take us by the hand and lead us with him. I don't want this simple sermon to be a funeral notice! It is simply the Gospel; it is life, simply saying to each other --- we are all vulnerable and we all have a door that the Lord will knock on one day."[24]

At the end of this first chapter, I would like to invite you to be grateful for the miracle of life. We are blessed because we love and experience his love as fire in the heart. The miracle of life is for each one of us, it is enough to recognize its beauty to realize that God is always present to help us become saints. We will all die one day, but before that day, we can grow in holiness.

Many people have died around the world because of this pandemic.

---

24   *Web-page: ACI Prensa, Vatican News (Translated from the English).*

Let's keep asking God to put an end, and let's also pray for all those who continue to suffer. When we live for God, we will die to everything around us and we will be blessed because in this world we will bring light to others. Thank you for being the light, thank you for being my light and for lighting my life with your prayer.

Blessed are you
you carry the light
in difficult times of pandemic,
you bear witness of perseverance
when everything seems
shadows, death and pain.
Blessed are you.

Towards Recovery

Afer I left the hospital, my province sent me to Marysville to start a long and painful therapy (Marysville is a Catholic center run by the sisters of St. Mary of Oregon).[1] Losing the ability to walk, eat, and cleanse myself, things we usually take for granted, was painful and embarrassing. I found myself helpless, I could compare this experience as to taking care of a baby. I had to let myself be taken care of, I often told the staff I could do it, but definitely couldn't. Again, I asked for help and they attentively helped me. God here was also teaching me a lesson---

Heavenly Father you have blessed me greatly. You have blessed me by sending me each of these nurses. You bless me and know what I need even before I ask. You give me confidence that you will continue to bless me in the future, without fail. Help me never to doubt your love and your providence. Allow me to use and share what you have given me for your glory.

---

1   *The Sisters of St. Mary of Oregon (SSMO) is a Roman Catholic religious congregation founded in 1886 in the state of Oregon. The sisters' convent is located in Beaverton. The Sisters provide lifelong learning opportunities through Bethany Center, which offers programs and lectures.*

Being at Marysville was a difficult but necessary process. There they bathed me and cleaned me, I was grateful for the help and I valued my fragility. God allowed me to learn to value the things I often ignored --- the simplest things like taking a shower, and the things I did throughout the day.

Marysville has a chapel and I had moments of prayer there. I enjoyed the silence and peace. I met God again and thanked him for life. I specifically gave thanks for getting sick with COVID because it helped me appreciate my frailty and learn to trust God more. Those moments of silence led me to feel I need others.

The illness, the silence, being in a coma, where I don't remember feeling anything, gave me time to rest with and in God and let Him take care of me. During all this time, the virus spread to all my organs, damaging my kidneys, lungs, heart, and **even my brain**, and yet I was still alive. I was not aware of what was happening. One day as I read the liturgy of the hours, I pause on Psalm 86 (*David's Psalm in the day of his affliction*). Because I identified myself with the words of the Psalmist; "Lord, hear my prayers, listen to my cry for help." While I read it my eyes moistened with gratitude for the gift that God placed on my lips. I have included all of Psalm 86 at the end of the book so you, too, can identify with it.

Incline your ear, LORD, and answer me,
for I am poor and oppressed.
Preserve my life, for I am devoted;
save your servant who trusts in you.

You are my God;
be gracious to me, Lord.
Gladden the soul of your servant;
to you, Lord, I lift up my soul.
Lord, you are good and forgiving,
most merciful to all who call on you.
LORD, hear my prayer;
listen to my cry for help.
On the day of my distress, I call to you,
for you will answer me.
None among the gods can equal you, O Lord.
All the nations you have made shall come
to bow before you, Lord,
and give honor to your name.
For you are great and do wondrous deeds;
and you alone are God.
Teach me, LORD, your way
that I may walk in your truth,
I will praise you with all my heart,
glorify your name forever, Lord my God.

Your mercy to me is great;
you have rescued me from the depths of the Grave.
Turn to me, be gracious to me;
give your strength to your servant;
Give me a **miracle** of your favor.

"Incline your ear, LORD, and answer me. Give your strength to your servant; Give me a **miracle** of your favor " As I read this sentence, my eyes moistened with gratitude for the gift of praying this psalm.

During the time I was critically ill with COVID, my brother priests and my family were suffering too. Some were filled with fear and uncertainty, but all had faith and hope. They did not stay in fear; they transformed the fear and uncertainty into faith and resolve to do more than sit by, they prayed, and they prayed a lot. Then prayer and the rosary had a privileged place. Without prayer, they would have been discouraged and uncertain of where God was taking me. But, although uncertain, they continued praying as Ilia Delio describes in her book:

> *Prayer is the energy of awakening to this radical presence of God. It is the breathing of God's Spirit in me that awakens me to the reality of my own existence. As I awaken to my own reality, I awaken to the reality of the whole of which I am part, the whole that is the universe itself. Although I am drawn to that which I cannot grasp, I am drawn to that which already holds me in the depth of my own beingness. As I am pulled into the power of God, my mind is filled with light and my being expands. Such is the power of contemplation.*[2]

---

2   *Delio, Ilia, The Hour of the Universe: Reflections of God, Science, and the Human Journey. Orbis Books, Maryknoll, New York. 2021.*

Being in a coma led me to contemplation, even if it seems unreal. I knew that I was not dead and that is why I can firmly say I had a dialogue with God, where He gave me the option to return to Him or return to earth --- I stayed even knowing it would take time to recover and that I would suffer in this lapsed time.

When we enter deep contemplation, we can have dialogues with God. Our founder Father Félix de Jesús Rougier used to say, *'Silence is the atmosphere where all virtues blossom.'* Silence brings us back to ourselves. That is why many do not want to be alone. Without external distractions, we are left vulnerable. Silencer helps us to muffle the noise in us, it calls us to authenticity. I was lucky to experience silence for three months while in a coma. You may wonder why I say, *'I was lucky.'* In response to you, I would simply say that I was not alone, God was with me. I decided to return to earth and finish my mission.

God never invades life, on the contrary, He respects our decisions, He has given us options to choose from, I continued in this life and God gave me one more opportunity, He respected my decision, I knew that the risk of making this decision would lead me to live with extreme difficulties, I did not know if I would recover one hundred percent, I would have to give up my responsibility as provincial, perhaps I could never communicate or even say mass, everything looked gray and I was full of uncertainty and so I returned.

The trauma of COVID left me very weak and broken, I was in this state for a long time, and thus I had the opportunity to speak with many friends. I had some short but very nice conversations and some longer and more in-depth talks with my relatives. Father Juan José González was sharing on the Facebook page about my situation and how my congregation and family were dealing with the pain of my condition. He thanked them for the prayers and reported my process. The total number of people who read this statement was over 54 thousand. My heart does not stop thanking God for this miracle and for the many prayers that people made for me.

I shared with my councilor how this was affecting me, she wisely asked me if before, when I was the provincial, was aware of how I influenced others and invited me to write a letter to that provincial (which was me) and share my feelings and what I asked now after COVID-19. When writing this letter, I realized things and details I was unaware of and these made me reflect even more on the importance of always examining my conscience. I want to share this letter with you because doing I also heal:

Roberto:

I am writing to you while you are in the past and I am in the present, the COVID-19 virus has not yet been discovered, the one that will leave millions of deaths around the world. You will get sick of this terrible disease and you will also be about to die, but you will manage **to cross the threshold of death**, thanks to the intercession of Father Félix de Jesús Rougier and thousands of people who will be praying for you in many parts of the world. You will be surprised to hear how your family; your brother priests and many people were distressed for you. You will be even more surprised when you learn that you wrote a book where you share your story and that this book has been read and will continue to be read by thousands of people around the world.

It is important that you know, so that you become aware of the love of so many people. Roberto many people love you and continue to love you and they show you with many details their affection. You should know that love moves mountains... I invite you to continue believing in love. Do not be afraid to love, even if it implies that you try, leave behind that victimization that usually characterizes you. How many times have people told you that they love you? You must believe it! You are worthy of affection, because you are valuable and worthy for them, they really love you and they are not hypocrites, as you sometimes think. They love you not because you are a priest, they love you as a friend and companion. They love you because you're close to them... don't keep thinking that they love you because you're a priest, that's also true, but it's not the main reason the friendship they profess for you.

I want to talk to you about your father Mateo, it is true that he did not show you his love... do not keep hurting yourself with feelings that he did not love you, that did not help you value yourself as a man, that is why you cried so many times alone when you walked among those eucalyptus trees... if your dad didn't tell you, it doesn't mean he didn't feel it, he loved you in his own way. He was tired of working in the lemon tree, of carrying so many bundles of lemons on his already sore back, so when he got home, he just wanted to have dinner and rest. He didn't think you just wanted to play or be close to him. Because of the little love you didn't feel from your father, and because he didn't have time for you, you didn't learn to defend yourself. You grew up fragile, shy and introverted, so at school you didn't have many friends, and you were teased. You came to think that there was something wrong with you, because they used to reject you, because they thought you were an idiot, or as they used to call you: "Nerd". Young people can be very cruel and you learned that painfully. But your mother Soledad, she did show you her love with many examples of tenderness and her love was extreme, from her you learned to be affectionate, but you haven't shown it, you must do it now. Your parents in heaven take care of you and they knew you would get sick with COVID and they were watching out for you.

Now you are a priest, you are mature, intelligent, respectable and responsible... do not make your feelings invisible, when you want to tell someone "I love you" say so. They will believe it because they know you are sincere and honest. You are not hypocritical in your comments, it is what I like most about you.

With this letter in the distance, I invite you to **paint your face with the color of hope,** let yourself be loved, do not get frustrated with nonsense. Enjoy life and enjoy your family and friends. Roberto, **life will change and you will feel your soul fly...** You will go through a very difficult time, after COVID you will spend a good time in recovery, when you have come out of it, enjoy yourself, love and do whatever you want as the apostle Saint John says in his letter... when you have finished reading this letter, I invite you to listen to this song by Diego Torres, *Color Esperanza* (the color of hope), you will like it:

I know what's in your eyes just by looking
That you are tired of walking and walking
and walk
Always turning in one place
I know the windows can be opened
Change the air is up to you
It will help you
worth it one more time
Know that you can
want it to be possible
get rid of fears
take them outside
Paint the face
Hope color
tempt the future
With the heart
It's better to get lost than never board
Better tempt yourself to stop trying
although you see
that it is not so easy to start
I know that the impossible can be achieved
That the sadness will one day go away
and so it will be
life changes and will change
you will feel
that the soul flies
to sing one more time

We all must heal from something as we go through life, and this healing is not instantaneous or quick. It can take a long time. The start of my recovery began in Marysville thanks to the care and attention I had there. When I said goodbye, I thanked each nurse and staff, and before leaving, I went to the chapel to thank God and say goodbye to Him. I felt the healing process with love. I thanked God for knowing this place, where care for the sick is a priority, not only because the place is Catholic, but the service is given with charity and love, Jesus being the main doctor. Let us remember that when Jesus was with us, he spent his entire time healing the sick.[3] We are all sick, if not in the body we can get sick in the soul because of sin, that is why we all need **recovery.** Jesus' priority was healing and preaching the good news. Jesus is the healer who gives hope to the world. When we experience illness, let us ask Jesus to heal us and thank him for the healing and recovery required and necessary. God has a beautiful plan for each one of us, I am glad of the plan He has for me.

I want to include in this first part of the book a writing from my niece Natalie Saldívar. While I was ill, my niece took an important role with fathers Juan José Gonzáles and Mario Rodríguez keeping people informed regarding my medical situation. Natalie was an intermediary with my family for the decisions that the province was making about my health. She also participated in decision-making with my brother priests and doctors about my condition and the steps to be taken regarding the decisions to be made. I thank Natalie, for her interest and affection; she

---

3   *We tend to think that God likes us to get sick and this is a lie. I have included a chapter entitled, "God's Will is to Heal."*

46

and each of my brother priests, especially Mario and Juan José, were incredible as were each one of my family members, brothers, sisters, nephews, cousins, and friends. I thank each one for their affection.

Here now the writing of my niece Natalie:

September 10, 2020, marks the day when our lives changed. By remembering all the painful, sad and anguished moments, it makes us reflect on the great miracle that God and Father Félix de Jesús Rougier have in process and, we, as his family, are his witness. It is difficult to remember those painful moments, but at the same time we are very grateful to God and Father Félix de Jesús Rougier. Thanks to them, we have our dear uncle in front of us, safe and sound.

The most beautiful thing about this story, which we will remember forever, is that it became a story of faith, hope, joy and reunion for the Saldívar family, because of the situation we live in, it united us more than ever. We are witnesses of a great miracle. My uncle Roberto is our miracle and our gift from God. We will remember November 20th forever. It is the day that God gave us a great blessing to have our uncle with us again. We will always be grateful to God for this great miracle.

When he was hospitalized, I wondered how I could help my uncle? He always helped me to get out of the most difficult moments that I have had to face in my life and now it was my turn to help him. I felt helpless, since he was hospitalized in Oregon, and I live in California. Not to mention, COVID-19 that further exacerbated the situation. Every night I prayed to God to enlighten me and give me strength to help my uncle. Prayer was my medicine and also my uncle's.

It all started when one day, I spoke to my mother, I felt her pain when I heard her voice, just by mentioning my uncle's name. Like me, she felt helpless not to be able to do something for her brother. She asked me to speak to the hospital to get information, and that's how I became an information bridge between the doctors and our family. The doctors and nurses were very kind to us. Every day they gave us a little summary about my uncle's health.

I remember that in the first call I made, I didn't ask anything, I just listened and started writing notes. Later, I began to inform my family through zoom in the family rosary, about the state of my uncle. Everyone thanked me for being the person who reported to them about my uncle's health. In that moment, it was where I discovered how to help. I know that family is and will always be very important. I knew that, in those moments, my uncle would have liked the family to know everything that was happening to him. Thus, my role as "Health Advocate" began.

My days consisted of talking in the morning and in the afternoon. The day before, I studied my notes I wrote the day before. In addition, I would read articles about patients in a coma, due to COVID. I did this to prepare myself, to ask good questions so that no details were missing. After each call, I would send my cousin Adriana a summary. She was in charge of reporting to the family by text message. She also took on a very important role since through her communication, was filtered to the whole family.

What the family went through was, in short, a roller coaster. Each day was a different diagnosis, but at the same time, a different hope. The cross that my uncle had to carry was a painful cross for him and his family. We were all part of each step of this path so full of pain. The days were unpredictable and long. The rosary united the family in pain and sadness, but at the same time in hope. Praying as a family became our coping mechanism to be able to assimilate everything that was happening. We always looked forward to the time of the rosary. It was a time when the family united in prayer, we prayed, we listened to the news and at the same time we saw my uncle.

My uncle, although unconscious, accompanied us every day in our rosaries through Zoom. As a family, we were very happy to see him, but also very sad to see him in the conditions he was suffering. I remember the first time we had the opportunity to see my uncle virtually during the rosary, it was a painful and crying moment. For the family, it was very shocking to see my uncle in the state he was. I immediately noticed faces filled with sadness. We were all silent and our eyes filled with tears.

It is very different to hear a report from the doctors and see reality with our own eyes. From that day on, we not only listened to the reports of the doctors, but we also lived it strongly when we saw the state in which he was. My family is very strong, but during this process I began to see how our wall began to collapse little by little. Every time we heard negative news from the doctors, our wall began to deteriorate. For me, it was very difficult to see my uncles, aunts, cousins suffer. My words of agreement became muffled phrases. The words did not come out, only tears. I asked God to give me strength to be able to face every bad news and communicate it to my family.

I remember that for me, it was a mental preparation every day. They were not only simple calls with the doctors and nurses but also, I had to make detailed notes. It was long to interpret the notes in English into Spanish, as well as to investigate everything that the nurses or doctors told me. I read the medical articles and also communicated with my friends who are nurses. Then I wrote my summary for the family report in detail. Those reports and calls that I had to make were very difficult because I did not know what news I had to communicate, I always hoped it was good and would fill us with happiness and hope, but other days were bad news and filled us with sadness.

One call that stuck in my mind was when the doctors reported to me that the probability that my uncle would survive was nil, that only a miracle could save him. Hearing those words, I felt great pain and my eyes filled with tears. I also remember that the doctor told us to start looking at options in case he did not survive. That we think about my uncle's wishes because he was not going to react. They basically told us to think about disconnecting him. As I bring this up with my family, I vividly noted the pain.

There was a long silence filled with sadness, tears, confusion and suffering. The faces of my family told me everything. I couldn't find the words to comfort them.

In all this, thank God that we always have the support of the other family, the Missionaries of the Holy Spirit, who always supported us and accompanied us in everything. They always comforted us, filled us with faith and hope and always knew what to say to make us feel better. They were also our medicine of faith and strength. But in particular, I had the honor of interacting with father Juan José and Father Mario, they consoled me and filled me with faith. They were always very attentive to me and filled me with strength. I had the fortune to win two friends to be able to get ahead in this difficult process. It is worth mentioning that it was not only them and us, but there were many people in different countries praying for his recovery.

Actually, I think that, for my uncle, all this he experienced will always be a test of faith, for which I quote again that phrase that he sent in a message before he was tubed, "God has a beautiful plan for me."

It is an honor to have a priest uncle and I thank God for sending us that beautiful gift, he is our strength and pillar of faith. When I found out that my uncle was infected with COVID, I was scared, but at the same time I knew that he was strong and was going to come out of this great battle. Above all, I knew that God was protecting him. I never thought that we would live what we had to live.

Imagine hearing the doctors tell us:

-His brain is not responding, its dead.

-We do not have a clear signal why the brain does not respond.

-We are extremely concerned about the condition of Father Roberto.

-We just don't know what else we can do.

-His eyes do not move together as they should.

-This situation he is in, is alarming.

-The chances of his returning to normal are very slim.

-Only a miracle can make a difference.

This is where this whole process took us, which began, and we never imagined how far it was going to go. Even after we were guaranteed that he would not survive and against all hope. After almost three months of being in a coma and **crossing the threshold of death**, he managed to wake up. Now awake, the doctors assured us that there would be damages because of everything that had affected him in his brain, lungs and kidneys.

That it was also likely that he would not move one or two of his feet and hands and that he also had to use dialysis for life. From there, this true miracle begins, even the doctors could not explain how it was that his kidneys began to work, and he did not need dialysis. That's when the merciful and miraculous God gave the Sáldivar family the best, irreplaceable gift, and that is to have our uncle, brother, friend, compadre and priest by our side again, safe and sound.

After living this miracle of life, we can only be eternally

grateful to God our Lord and follow his communion as a show of faith to give testimony of the power of prayer and say like Saint Elizabeth Ann Seton: **"God is mine and I am his."**

Reading my niece's reflection, I wondered, had God wanted me not to continue living, what silent tears would have questioned God?

My family loves Jesus; each has a strong faith. They all wanted me to live. But before their desire was the YES to the will of God; God is always first, although it might imply me dying.

The months I was in the hospital were marked by a great and terrible "fact"; my sickness by the COVID virus would separate me from my Community and my family, and doctors were certain I would die. My niece gathered all the information possible to share with my family. She intended to have the family informed for them to become conscious of the reality that the possibly of death was real. She was prepared to learn everything she needed to answer all questions. Her reflection proves this point, and I am grateful to her.

Life does not end with death because eternal life awaits us; we are not alone. It is not as if we are in a small ship and at the mercy of the waves. We are in a big ship with full power to navigate all storms.

As I reflect on my life and how close I came to dying --- I now better understand Jesus overcoming death --- He rose to defeat it; and our experience of death will be for us only a process that leads us to freedom... the book of Wisdom says: "Teach me to number my days and I will reach the wisdom of the heart" (Ps 90,12). Jesus himself says: "... be careful because you do not know the day or the hour" (Mt 25,13). The Italian priest Gualberto Bormolini, when asked about death, replies: "Don't worry about it, ask yourself rather, if there is life before death." He also said in an interview with Parabola magazine:

"There are two things that make a wonderful life; limitations,
and not knowing when we are going to die."[4]

These two phrases made me think about the importance of enjoying life, which I am already doing. I invite you to prepare for death. Saint Alphonsus Maria de Liguori invites us to make this a daily practice.

Saint Augustine's insight on faith in eternal life can illuminate; he wrote about the comments made when a child is born, "…many hypotheses are made; perhaps he is beautiful, perhaps he is ugly; maybe he will be rich, maybe he will be poor; maybe he will live a long life, maybe not … But it is said of no one; maybe he will die or maybe he will not die. This is the only absolutely certain thing in life. When we know that one is sick (terminally), we say, 'Poor man, he will die; he is condemned, there is no remedy. But shouldn't we say the same of one who is born? *'Poor man, he must die, there is no remedy, he is doomed!" What does it matter if it's a little longer or a little shorter? Death is the fatal disease contracted at birth'.*

COVID has allowed me to look at death from Father Guidalberto's perspective. The thought of Saint Augustine also helped me; I am condemned to die because I was born. What matters the time of life I have left to live. I will die --- I accept it, and I am at peace. Now I share my feelings without fear.

I enjoy what I do, what I eat and drink. That is the gift that COVID-19

---

4   *Bi-monthly magazine 'Parabola,' Spring 2022, April 30, 2022.*

left me. I am grateful and happy. I could not imagine that my life change with a pandemic. I'm not the same, I feel better. Life is given to us one day at a time and each day must be lived to the fullest, let us not allow any day to be wasted, --- this is how Gilbert Keith Chesterton sees it in his poem:

> *Here dies another day*
> *During which I have had eyes, ears, hands*
> *And the great world round me;*
> *And with tomorrow begins another.*
> *Why am I allowed two?*

Why are we allowed two? I have great admiration for G.K. Chesterton and I answer something he already knows --- because it's grace, God "makes his sun rise on the bad and the good and causes rain to fall on the just and the unjust" (Matthew 5:45). Living in a broken world, today I convalescing thank a new beginning that offers two. It is my reminder that God loves me. Every new day is an opportunity to leave the past behind. No matter what darkness you faced yesterday, today we can say with the prophet Jeremiah:

> *The LORD's acts of mercy are not exhausted, his compassion*
> *is not spent; They are renewed each morning— great is your*
> *faithfulness! The LORD is my portion, I tell myself, therefore*
> *I will hope in him. The LORD is good to those who trust in*
> *him, to the one that seeks him; It is good to hope in silence*
> *for the LORD's deliverance. It is good for a person, when*

young, to bear the yoke (Lamentations 3: 22-27).

God did not have to bless us with these contrasting times and seasons, but He did so in his grace. Tonight, look at the moon and thank God you, too, can answer G.K. Chesterton Why are we allowed two?

Vulnerability

V ulnerability is the quality or state of being exposed to the possibility of being attacked or harmed, either physically or emotionally. COVID physically attacked and harmed me because I was vulnerable. I was the prey of its claws; I was defenseless and I was an easy prey for this disease, I was lucky that God was with me. I was aware of my weakness, and I held firm to him because I have a purpose and a mission to accomplish. Mario Benedetti in his book *Rincón de Haikus* underlined, *'Who would have said, the really weak never give up.'* [1]

In the book of Job, we read: "How fragile is the human being! How short is life, so full of difficulties and sufferings! We bloom like a flower and then we wither; we disappear like a passing shadow" (Job 14, 1). This disease would not change my decision to live, even in my fragility and my vulnerability I would not give up, God was by my side, that is why I did not give up; From my childhood I was insecure, I remember that I sought the company of my sister Silvia because with her I felt protected, but Silvia wanted to get closer to my older sisters and I took up her time. I would have sought the company of my brother Rodrigo, who was older than Silvia but he had a independent character and never allowed me to

---

1   *Benedetti, Mario. Rincón de Heikus, Editorial Sudamericana. Buenos Aires.*

get close to him.

Besides being insecure, I was always very shy about many things, but now, years later, God gave me the strength, the security to overcome cowardice, I would fight against COVID, I would win the battle against this disease.

Love and suffering open up to the experience of the unknown and this is always difficult to combine, but if we do not live them together, we will not know what is essential in life. That is why Jesus invites us to love our Lord "with all your heart, with all your soul, with all your mind and with all your strength... and love your neighbor as yourself" (Mark 12, 30-31). Interpreted in this way to love with all our strength will imply suffering. This is how love works, yielding our will. When we suffer, we have the option to remain in it or open ourselves to life. If we choose life then we choose love, and love helps us accept the terrible feeling of loneliness, separation and fear...

We have been created with love to love, the heart beats in and for love, but this is always in suffering because suffering detaches the heart from the self, and this is always a mystical experience. Karl Rahner (1904-1984) prophesied it like this "In this century Christian of the future will be a mystic or will not exist at all."[2] We come to Jesus through mysticism because the heart of God is only experienced in mystery. Suffering is the best means to live mysticism because through it we learn to renounce. Suffering may feel wrong, absurd, unfair, physically painful, or simply out

---

2   *Bucey, Candem, Karl Rahner: Great Thinkers (A series), P&R Publishing Company, Phillipsburg New Jersey 2019.*

of our comfort zone. Accepting suffering helps us transform pain. If we accept suffering, then we can all be mystics, as Karl Rahner says.

Suffering can lead us to bitterness or compassion. To compassion because we join the feeling of God who is compassionate and merciful, or to bitterness when, by not accepting pain, we fill ourselves with it. We should all pray for the grace of compassion. This is the true meaning of the phrase "deliver us from evil" in the Our Father. We are not asking to avoid suffering. Rather we should pray that when the great trials come, God will not abandon us.

The heart beats approximately 103.680 times in 24 hours; in each beat it can open up a space for love. People who have never loved or who have never suffered, metaphorically speaking, will usually try to control their heartbeat. Jesus commands us to "love our neighbor as ourselves," and connects the two great commandments of love of God and love of neighbor, saying they are "like" each other (see Matthew 22:40). Often, we think that this means loving our neighbor with the same amount of love, as much as we love ourselves. Actually, it means it must be the same source.

But before the tests there is always the ego; it is always there in an obvious way we cannot ignore. We resist any correction and any advice given to us and we judge. We must be humble and vulnerable in accepting our limitations. To look in the mirror and see who we are, then we can see others authentically.

When we all crave physical touch and community, we sometimes forget to do just that. We need to 'un-mask' from indifference and reach out in simple loving ways to each other, a smile, a cheery greeting, a note written to someone living alone. The virtue we all need to reach for these COVID days is to TRUST the Lord.

In this book, I have tried to 'unmask' and tell my story honestly and simply. As I deal with the trauma that COVID left in me, my counselor is now challenging me metaphorically to remove to my 'facemask,' and live barefaced, open and vulnerable. I have exposed 'pieces of myself' as I journey with the Lord through this critical time of recovery. I am not perfect, nor do I have a perfect life. My trust is in the Lord who continues to guide me to complete recovery. Feeling vulnerable also made me limited in many things and I needed the help of many people, this was the best lesson of my life.

Sadly, many are ignorant of what is going on around them and may even deliberately decide not to notice the suffering of others. They avoid feeling sympathy for anyone, strongly encourage stupidity, ignorance and lack of empathy for others, and take pride in not being moved by anyone's suffering. These people are usually unaware of world problems, poverty, deforestation, climate change and global warming, etc. They have created a tough skin and then socialize with people like them.

We need more truth to offset the facade of perfect lives we think we live. We need more stories about the fears, the tears, the struggles for these often-indifferent people to let go of their ignorance and lack of empathy.

All this came to my mind and to my heart because after the hospitalization, I felt vulnerable, useless, empty and tired, I was anxiously looking for solutions and answers to the why this pandemic, I did not get answers or any relief. This was a disturbing feeling. I had difficulty remembering who I was and what I did; I even forgot the parts of the Mass to where I could not do the physical gestures. I needed to read, to distract me from the evil thoughts of feeling useless and unwanted. I suffered; it was difficult. I cried many times because I felt lonely. Loneliness now had a different skin; it was crude; hard, it felt different like never before. I had to let go of these thoughts and feelings, so I walked as much as I physically, besides, therapy required it. I wanted to see the sky, feel the sunshine, to feel I was still alive; I wanted the breeze of the air to revive me, so I would once again feel in control. But as soon as I walked, I got tired and once again I was miserable. I wanted to see the sky, feel the warmth of the sun, feel I was still alive; I wanted the breeze and the air to revive me, so I would feel in control again, but the opposite happened like a flame that went out... I listened to music and some songs seemed written for me... in particular, one song by Lauren Strahm (Fleurie) that made me cry:

I know it hurts
It's hard to breathe sometimes
These nights are long
You've lost the will to fight
Is anybody out there?
Can you lead me to the light?
Is anybody out there?
Tell me it'll all be alright
You are not alone
I've been here the whole time singing you a song
I will carry you

I know you can't remember how to shine
Your heart's a bird without the wings to fly
Is anybody out there?
Can you take this weight of mine?
Is anybody out there?
Can you lead me to the light?
You are not alone
I've been here the whole time singing you a song
I will carry you[3]

Days passed and the certainty grew within me I would not recover. Every afternoon, when the sun no longer warmed my soul, it also hurt. Entering the night, my whole body felt itchy, that stupid itch prevented me from sleeping. During long hours I asked, Why Lord... why is this happening? Why this itching? Should I offer it? Yes, I said it many times and decided not to scratch it, but I couldn't resist and scratched even more. The next morning when I made my bed, I could see the sheets with blood on them.

I wanted to accept all this with love and offer it to my Lord, accepting this cross and sharing it with Him, I remembered Conchita and Father

---

3 *Lauren Strahm, better known by her stage name Fleurie, is an American singer born in Nashville, Tennessee. Carry You from "Songs of Razor and Tie," Maggie Eckford Publishing, Collapsible Soul Music.*

Félix, I thought of the servant of God Chiara Lubich[4], which I accidentally found out about him with a letter I read I didn't know how it got to me. I would like to share it with you:

Lord, when they speak of love, most people perhaps think of something that is always the same. Yet, how varied love is! Lord, I remember how I met you. I didn't worry then about how to love you. Maybe because it was you who came to me, and you who took care to fill my heart. I remember virtually burning with love for you. Certainly, I felt the dragging burden of my humanity, but through your grace I understood already then, a little of who I was and who you were. I understood that the flame in my heart was your gift. Then you showed me a way to find you. "Under the cross, under every cross," you would tell me, "I am there. Embrace it and you will find me." You said this to me many times. While I don't remember your reasoning, I do know that you convinced me. As each suffering arrived, I thought of you, and with my will I said yes. The cross, however, remained: an inner darkness, a heartrending pain --- how many crosses in our life![5]

---

4   *Silvia Chiara Lubich (1920-1918) Italian teacher and author, founder of the Focolare movement which is now in many parts of the world.*

5   *Hearne, Jerry. Heaven on Earth – Meditations and Reflections. New City Press, Hyde Park, NY.*

This painful experience gave me a cross I lived in a hospital bed and felt like an altar. I still feel this cross; it is like a knot tightening hope and leaving me helpless; feeling as vulnerable as when I got lost in the market at six. I cried because I couldn't find my parents, I wanted them to be here caressing me and taking care of me, sitting next to them eating sugary fried noodles.

I want to return to my occupations, but my brain stops me, and my mind says, I am the Provincial, I have responsibilities, and my brain orders me NO! Accept yourself as you are. My mind and brain negotiate. Thanks to Father Mario Rodríguez, who was my shoulder where I rest during this martyrdom time, he carried the responsibilities of the province, thank you, God, for being so good! Thank you, Mario, for being there, close.

The days went on, after the day followed the night, the same routine… all I heard was the word 'recovery,' every visit to the hospital, every visit to the doctor, every therapy was to recover. I was sick of hearing this word repeatedly. 'You need to recover; you have to recover, first you must recover, to send you to another community you will have to recover, ---recovery, recover, recover, 'We will have to evaluate you after your recovery', was the comment of my superior, 'then we will decide'.

I can't live my life recovering, can I? Once recovered, what will happen then? For the first time I realized what it feels like to be disabled. Being unable to drive and every time I left the house, I was forced to pay attention to the parking signs because when they parked the car further away; I had to walk more and it was exhausting for me; 'you should park closer' was my comment, 'walking will help you recover' was often the response. If walking was difficult, it was much more difficult going up and down stairs, thank God for the railings. Wow, before I didn't realize that people need to hold on to them to step safely before I would have done it running up or down without any problem. How I missed doing that!

Many people seek approval from the outside to feel good, but this will never fix what's on the inside. That's why a true human connection can offer more guidance than a plan that promises success. We need to validate our own human experience.

It takes great willpower to recognize weakness, but it takes greater strength to ask for help. An even greater force is needed to change. Being authentic invites others to do the same. Create a space to express and share vulnerability. The willingness to see and acknowledge our weaknesses is how we take advantage of our vulnerability, which creates connection. To be vulnerable is to be susceptible to being hurt.

Now I feel broken and unfinished. I experience depression like never before. Today, as I write in this book, I feel lost, exhausted, sad, disabled and with no place to go... for the first time, I have asked for help, and I have also been scolded. 'You are like a teenager; you don't put limits on your comments," said a brother. It was a simple observation, but his words were devastating because of what I was going through with COVID. I'm sure you never thought your comment would be so hurtful. I took refuge in music and I don't know if it helped or worsened my feeling more down, I share this song[6] that also touched my heart:

Some days I spin till I'm sick

---

6 *Dora Pereli / Shelby Benjamin. Feel Ok © Distrokid*

Counting time I have missed
I get weak
I get restless
I get lost in it
And I don't like my bridges burned
But lessons lived are lessons learned
I get low
I get lonely
I get lost in it
I'm a million little pieces
Cause I wanna be believed in
I'm a rhyme without a reason
And I can't seem to find a purpose
I just want to feel okay
If you hear me out there
This will be my broken prayer
I need change
I need something
To feel hope again
I'm a million little pieces
Cause I wanna be believed in'
I'm a rhyme without a reason
I can't seem to find a purpose
I just want to feel okay

Feeling so vulnerable is how I took more refuge in the Spirituality of the Cross, in the precious blood of Jesus (see I Peter 1, 19-22). From which he rescued us all from an unproductive, meaningless life, redeeming us. We all need salvation, therefore the need to be redeemed (see Galatians 3, 13).[7]

Never have I felt so weak and miserable. I had time to read a book of poems and I identified with a poem written by Luis Alberto Ambroggio titled **Poverty**[8] from his book, *'En el Jardín de los Vientos* (In the Garden of the Winds):'

When I'm down
and little by little without desire
I touch the bottom of myself
and I feel nothing
as if I ceased to exist
the world will collapse
and I share very deeply
in the scarcity of the soul
being dispossessed
of that human misery
I want to enjoy poverty

---

7   *"Christ redeemed us from the curse of the law, making himself a curse for us, for the Scripture says: Cursed is everyone who hangs on a tree, so that the blessing of Abraham might come to the Gentiles in Christ Jesus, and by faith we might receive the Spirit of Promise."*

8   *Ambroggio, Luis Alberto, (Pobreza: Reston, Virginia, 26 de abril de 1975). En el Jardín de los Vientos. Obra Poética (1974-2014). Academia Norteamericana de la Lengua Española (ANLE), 2014, New York, NY, Pg. 28, (Translated from the Spanish).*

who does not know cravings
and value what is
because it has nothing
flying over these things
of my imprisoned life.

Escape in music and **poetry**
attain the highest greatness.
I would like to return to what I had
when I had nothing
just the thought, the look
or the word happiness
and what is not seen or touched
what is not bought in the market.
who could teach me
to ignore what I lack?

My vulnerability has stopped my facade, and instead, God's goodness has brought me healing and comfort in this battle I waged. Saint Teresa of Lisieux felt the same, although I am far from being in her place, this is what she experiences and writes in her diary 'Story of a Soul'...

> *Oh, how happy I am to see myself imperfect and to be in need of God's mercy so much even at the moment of my death.*[9]

9　*Therese of Lisieux, Story of a Soul, trans. John Clarke, OCD, Washington, DC: ICS Publications, 1996. epilogue. P. 267.*

Embracing our 'vulnerability' and walking with it will help us see ourselves as we are, 'imperfect' and in need of God, it will even help us at the time of our passing away. St. Teresa of Avila had struggle to understand how it was possible that God could actually be working in her life while she continued to be so imperfect and weak. Personally, I feel the same way but definitely I am much more sinful. My weaknesses are obvious. Sometimes I feel I haven't been attentive to God and the many times He has bestowed on me graces I haven't acknowledged. Now I know it was His way to tell me to be more attentive to the dangers around me.

There is a poem written by Alexandra Farbiarz More "The Force of Vulnerability".[10] I would like to share it with you…

When everything seems to fall
when exhaustion exhausts you even more than you thought possible,
when nothing seems what you thought it was,
when sadness peeks through the window of your eyes
without you being able to hide it,
vulnerability comes and embraces you
and it is also she who tells you

«Here you continue with me
as usual
learning from me,
walking way

---

10   *Alexandra Farbiarz: alexandrafarbiarz.com, 2021*

and knowing that I am
my own reverse,
what you work through me,
the trust.
You don't have to run away from me
kindly accompany me
and you will see that the earth
that you feel lost under your feet
It's just a path that follows
for new paths
and a way to meet
new colors of my reverse»

My family has seen my disability and has sympathized and continues to pray for me. They are not focused only on my recovery as the others insist. They pray, and they know that God is working in me, they support what I do. They remember the miracle that God did. Let me fill your hearts and minds as you acknowledge the challenging circumstances I experienced.

To bring redemption to our vulnerability is the aim. We need to lift eyes to God in hope. God has more promises to us; these will bring us comfort. COVID made my ears to be more attentive and listen to the struggles of others and pray for them. Weakness and vulnerability have reminded me that God is sufficient.

Will I recover? YES… although sometimes I think NO, because of how traumatic this experience has been. Having had brain damage and traumatic injuries that affected brain neurons, the doctors assured me that I would never walk again, eat by myself and even less drive a car (this was not even within the possibilities, I mentioned it because it is important for me). The symptoms that would appear because of this damage would be immediate and would be obvious to those who were with me, I would have difficulty concentrating, coordinating my ideas and thoughts. That's why I started therapy right away at the Marysville Rehab Center doing various exercises. I had difficulty concentrating and coordinating my ideas. I was easily disoriented within the rehabilitation center itself. I also did not reason well, because it took me a while to process my ideas to answer what they asked me. I had to solve crossword puzzles and various exercises presented. Multitasking was super difficult. As part of the therapy, I had to keep an agenda that included the calendar. They said that I would have communication problems and this would cause frustration not only for me but also for my brothers. This would lead to conflicts for not understanding or understanding what I was told or ordered. This would also make it difficult to hold conversations and participate in them; this led me to continue with therapies at St. Vincent Providence hospital for many months and on many occasions, I received the therapists in my home to receive instructions and therapies.

My life has had a succession of ups and downs. I continue to trust that God has a reason for the adverse events I have experienced and continue to experience. Each experience, each suffering, has led me to an experience and a teaching. So says Psalm 34: 19: "God is close to those whose hearts are broken, He saves the sinking spirits." Teilhard de Chardin invites me to **Worship and Trust:** [11]

Do not worry about the difficulties of life,
for your ups and downs, for your disappointments,
for your more or less bleak future.
Want what God wants.
Offer him in the midst of concerns and difficulties
the sacrifice of your simple soul that,
Above all,
accept the designs of his providence.
It doesn't matter if you consider yourself frustrated
if God considers you fully realized,
to your taste.
Lose yourself blindly trusting in that God
who wants you for himself.
And that will come to you, even if you never see it.
Think that you are in their hands,
all the more tightly grasped,
the more down and sadder you are.
Live happy. I beg. Live in peace.
Let nothing alter you.
Let nothing be able to take away your peace.

---

11   *Dúplex, André, Orar con Pierre Teilhard de Chardin (Praying with Teilhard de Chardin), Traducción Isidro Arias Pérez, Editorial Sal Terrae, 2014. Cantabria, España (Translated from the Spanish).*

Not mental fatigue. Nor your moral failings.
make it sprout,
and always keep on your face,
a sweet smile,
reflection of which the Lord
continually leads you.
And in the depths of your soul place,
first of all,
as a source of energy and criterion of truth,
everything that fills you with the peace of God.
Remember:
everything that depresses and worries you is false.
I assure you in the name
of the laws of life
and the promises of God.
So, when you feel heavy, sad,
love and trust.

For 19 months I have not driven depriving myself of freedom and independence. It has not been easy to face this reality. My brother priests have taken me everywhere, especially to medical appointments, but they have not always been available. I have asked friends for help to take me to various places and they have always been available and happy to do so. I thank them for these tokens of affection. Other times I asked for Uber. Now the good news: against all odds, I have made incredible progress in my neurological therapies, God has been good; now I have passed the driving test and the person who accompanied me has congratulated me, commenting that after knowing my medical history I have driven so well and she was surprised that I could not obtain the medical license to drive beforehand. *'What the doctors claimed was not true,'* she told me with a smile. *'God has a unique plan for you'* was her last comment, this comment surprised me because as an employee of *"Bridges for Independence"* they rarely talk about God.

It has been a long journey with God and with my vulnerability. What follows will not be easy, I cannot recover just by putting on a *'band-aid,'* as a priest, I have helped many people It is the priest's mission, to go where help is needed. There are many spiritual needs and family needs; there should be a balance and we should stop scolding and focus more on giving comfort and hope. I need my parishioners; in this life we walk together through difficult things and pleasant things. There are seldom quick or simple solutions to life's problems, but we can look to a mighty, merciful, loving and all-sufficient Father who has loved us through his Son.

I recently had an evaluation with the Provincial Council, they wanted to know how I was progressing in my recovery. My brothers from my community were also present. I remember how I felt during this meeting where they listened. I was uncomfortable; my words were, *'I don't need to be evaluated.'* Inside I thought this looked like a test; they didn't want to know how I was feeling physically and spiritually. Then I told them, *'This could have been done in a conversation or in a personal dialogue with any of you who were interested in my situation.'* I would like them to understand how difficult it is for me to be in this adverse situation. I just came back from the dead after months of suffering. Their reasoning and comments did not communicate empathy. So, I told them, '*I know it will take time to fully recover, I am aware of that. I have patiently accepted my illness and my vulnerability because it was difficult. I am working on being the person I always was. I know that God has a plan for me...*'

In this 'assessment' I spoke openly. They had other questions and even argued among themselves because my superior asked them on a scale of 1 to 100 what percentage they saw I had advanced. Thank God they did not respond because they immediately commented that it was an out of place question and only the doctors had the right to answer. Talking helped me mentally deal with this treatment.

In this 'assessment' I spoke openly. They had other questions and even argued among themselves because my superior asked them on a scale of 1 to 100 what percentage they saw I had advanced. Thank God they did not answer because they immediately commented that it was an unfair question and only the doctors had the right to answer. Talking helped me mentally deal with this treatment. I try to follow the example of Jesus and transform the 'bad/painful' into good, working hard to recover what had been taken from me by the COVID virus. God asks me to respond with love to suffering and mistreatment of any kind. This whole recovery process has been difficult, but prayer has made it possible. I know that God is with me. I pray that everyone gains an understanding of illness and "disability" and sees the person afflicted with illness as a person of value...

How good, sufficient, kind, persistent and merciful is God. His grace makes us aware of our need for Him. In the hospital, I called him and became dependent on him, and he reminded me of his love.

Embracing our various weaknesses so the power of God can be manifested is what helps others grow in their faith. It's the reminder we all need on a daily basis. God is good. God loves us. God is enough. No matter how weak or vulnerable you are, you can look to Christ, who from the cross joins your pain, affliction or need that you are going through at any time, and whose grace should be sufficient. God perfects you in weakness (see 2 Corinthians 12:9). So now ask yourself, do you love God? Have you asked him to love you? Vulnerability is allowing oneself to be loved by God; this is how Blessed Concepción Cabrera de Armida explains it:

> *Letting ourselves be loved by him? is to receive his approach of love even if it embarrasses us. Letting ourselves be loved by him is to open ourselves to all the demand of love. It means looking at him when he wants us to look at him. It means loving him as he wants us to love him. It means being silent when he needs us to be silent. It means speaking when he is listening. Listening when he is speaking. Being in spiritual darkness when this pleases him and enjoying his light when he sends it. In a word, letting ourselves be loved means losing our soul in Jesus and being a flawless mirror that reflects his glance.[12]*

---

12   *Cabrera de Armida, Concepción. What Jesús is Like. St. Paul/Alba House. Staten Island, NY. 2008.*

The spiritual journey begins by accepting the grace of God and will continue in the same way. Saint Francis de Sales tells us... Good works are of such value that heaven itself is given to us for them; but it is not because they come from us and from our heart, but because they are stained with the blood of the Son of God.[13]

We have received life as a gift; we are unique, precious, worthy of God, so we can offer our lives as a gift and sacrifice. Our vulnerability makes us aware of our limitedness, what more beautiful use can be made of life than to give it in our fragility, and with love to the Creator who gave it to us out of love? The words I say at Mass at the offertory about the bread and the wine can also be yours: "From your goodness we have received this life of ours; we present it to you so that it may become a living sacrifice, holy, pleasing to you" (cf. Romans 12: 1).

---

13   *Francis de Sales, Treatise on the Love of God, trans. Dom Henry Benedict Mackey, OSB, (Rockford, Il: TAN Publishers, 1997). Pp 478-81.*

Félix de Jesús Rougier

Three days after arriving at Marysville, I had a dream with Father Félix de Jesús Rougier; he was sitting in the first bench of a beautiful church surrounded by stained glass windows. Father Félix listened attentively as I preached. I shared that God had mercy on me and allowed me to continue living. At that moment, I thanked Father Félix for his intercession because through him, God gave me back the gift of my life. Father Felix, with a smile gratefully approved what I was sharing. His smile touched me. I do not remember any more from this dream, but the important thing happened afterwards when I woke up.

In the room, I felt the presence of Father Félix, I was curious to turn on the light to see if he was there, but I held back. I thought that maybe I was imagining it. What I am sure of is this dream confirmed what many people had asked for --- many were praying to Father Félix for God to perform a miracle; I was unaware of this, but many parishioners asked for prayers for my recovery, they ignored the seriousness because I was practically given up for dead. This request even reached churches where I am a stranger; Churches as far away as cities in Mexico, Brazil, and as far away as Israel, someone let me know that a person wrote my name on a small piece of paper and glued it to a candle he placed inside the tomb of Our Lord Jesus Christ; When I found out, I related the dream and confirm that Father Félix was interceding for me.

Now I would like to include something brief about the life of Father Félix de Jesús Rougier, since he was the founder of the congregation of the **Missionaries of the Holy Spirit**[1] in 1914:

> Father Felix was the first of the children of Benedict Rougier and Luisa Olanier; he was born on December 17, 1859, in a small town called Meilhaud in the Province of Auvergne, France.
>
> At the school, where Felix was studying while still a child, the children gathered in the main courtyard one day because a bishop wanted to speak to them (there were about 400 children). He was a missionary bishop who came from the Samoa Islands (Oceania). Among the things he told them, he summed up saying: "The harvest is abundant, and the workers are few. I have come to knock on the doors of your faith and your generosity. Are there any of you who want to accompany me to the missions in Oceania? Raise your hand".
>
> Father Félix looked around him and no one raised his hand. Then he

---

1   *The Congregation of the Missionaries of the Holy Spirit was founded by Venerable Fr. Félix de Jesús Rougier and Blessed Concepción Cabrera de Armida on December 25, 1914, in Mexico City. Both founders are in Canonization Process in addition to being recognized for the works they carried out. The congregation is organized into three provinces: the Province of Félix de Jesús Rougier (northern Mexico and Italy), the Province of Guadalupe (southern Mexico, South America and Spain) and the Province of Cristo the Priest (United States).*

felt an irresistible movement inwardly, but he waited a second; he couldn't resist anymore and raised his hand.

On September 24, 1878, Father Felix, who was then 18 years old, began his novitiate in the Congregation of Marist Fathers who attended the missions in Oceania.

At the novitiate, after having placed his right hand in a river of cold water, he became ill with deforming arthritis, and for several weeks the pain spread and covered his entire hand. Despite his illness, he was accepted to continue his formation as a novice and thus made his first vows on September 24, 1879. On October 7, he began his studies in philosophy. Two years went by. The arthritis also invaded the left leg. His vocation was in danger, and this made him suffer.

In those days Saint John Bosco, the founder of the Salesians, whose fame of holiness spread throughout Europe, arrived in the city. Father Félix's mother was a Salesian benefactor and took him to pray for him, Saint John Bosco laid his hands on his head. He prayed for his health and for his vocation. Within a few days, Father Félix Rougier was cured of arthritis. Illness was no longer an obstacle to his vocation. After a while, he was healed.

After his ordination, Father Félix was sent to Colombia, even though he wanted to be sent to Oceania because that was what prompted him to raise his hand when he was a child in that courtyard in response to the bishop's request. Colombia later began a war for Independence and after the difficulties that ensued, Father Félix was transferred to Mexico to the church of Our Lady of Lourdes. This was a parish destined for the French immigrants who lived in Mexico City, there he was appointed superior and pastor on February 17, 1902.

Although everything was going well, Father Félix did not feel inner peace; he was looking for a change, something that would indicate what God wanted of him. He was looking for something that would make him feel it was there where he belonged. Then he made a novena to the Holy Spirit, asking the Spirit to deign to call him to a greater perfection and clarify his discernment. In his diary, he wrote:

I feel the need for
a profound change in life,
for a greater surrender to God.

In God's response to that desire and that prayer, on February 4, 1903, a meeting took place with Concepción Cabrera de Armida and Father Felix that began a new stage in his spiritual life. God intercedes for us daily and works miracles in the world every day; the miracle of life being the most precious. Father Felix gave his life and his heart to Jesus so this meeting with Concepcion was no accident of fate. We know that Jesus always prepares us and leads us to those people who can help us grow in grace. For Father Félix, that person was a woman: Conchita – a simple lady born in San Luis Potosí, Mexico, on December 8, 1862. Her school education was sparse because she spent her childhood in the countryside at the ranches of her family. When she met Father Félix de Jesús Rougier, Conchita was 41 years old, a widow, taking care of and educating her nine children. In Father Félix's diary, we read:

Mrs. Cabrera told me that it was necessary for me to come out of this spiritual lethargy in which I found myself, to give myself to God with decision, and to start a new life. In that conversation, my life turned to new horizons. From that day on, my future took on another color. My heart was inflamed with love for the Cross, now it seems more desirable and more luminous. I feel changed and I have turned out to lead a life of more perfection. I love my Lord and think of Him constantly.

As this passed, he had the certainty that his meeting with Concepcion Cabrera de Armida was the work of God and his vocation was to be the founder of the Missionaries of the Holy Spirit. This certainty came from several sources; the main source was the inner light that God communicated to him, but also, he had the certainty of the sanctity of life he had seen and verified in Conchita.

Father Félix had a special affection for Jesus whom he addressed with great tenderness because he loved very much, he was obedient, especially to his superiors. We can learn a lot from this holy priest; let us love Jesus doing good with joy, there we will be more humane and charitable. This doesn't have to be difficult; it is easy if we intend to do good. Meister Eckhart put it nicely when he says, "God is the newest thing there is, the youngest thing, and if we are united to God, we become new again."[2]

---

2   *Meditations with Meister Eckhart, intro, and trans. Matthew Fox (Santa Fe, NM: Bear and Company, 1983), 32*

United to God we can do a lot of Good.

When Father Félix was in Barcelona, exiled by his superiors, he wrote a prayer to Jesus (May 31, 1904). May this prayer help you to love Jesus:

Your love, oh Jesus, is my love!
Oh, my beloved Jesus, your love is my love...
I don't want anything else, neither in this world nor in another...
I am confused by these implausibility's
I'm scared, I feel so bad!
But on the other hand, you being
so strong and so compassionate and so loving!
Your love is my love
What a comfort to be able to say that, and, by your grace, to feel it!
Oh yes, yes, my Life; forever, until the last breath,
I want what you want, I want what you love,
reject what you reject, hate what you hate!
I give myself totally to your most holy will.
I am yours and yours forever.

I appreciate the prayers of many people who asked for a miracle. May Mary our mother intercedes for each one and with Father Félix say: **"With Mary everything, without her nothing."**

Hope and Suffering

G od wants our salvation, "...he sees our needs, our pain, our struggle, he sees the afflicted heart and wants to give it strength" (cf., Psalms 38,10). It is this loving, merciful God, to whom we must give gratitude, praise and adoration. God is always waiting to receive us, no matter how many times we reject Him, like the father in the parable of the prodigal son,[1] he will wait for us at the entrance of the road to receive us when we want to arrive and then he will throw a grand celebration. This is a moving and comforting vision of God. God is a close lover.

Pain and suffering must not extinguish happiness. Life without energy and without meaning discourages... then darkness arises.

We have a generous God; He is always there for us --- it is as simple

---

1   Luke 15: 11-32 (In particular verses 22-24: "His father ordered his servants, 'Quickly bring the finest robe and put it on him; put a ring on his finger and sandals on his feet. Take the fattened calf and slaughter it. Then let us celebrate with a feast, because this son of mine was dead, and has come to life again; he was lost and has been found.' Then the celebration began"). Reflection: Imagine God the Father spotting you at the distance, running towards you, hugging you and covering you with kisses. Be moved by God's incredible love for you. Let it His tenderness and that joy invade you. See how God hardly allows you to excuse yourself and how He completely restores you. Do you really feel that God offers his forgiveness and unconditional love, or are you the one who often send negative or hurtful messages to yourself and wallow in your sin, in your failures? (From God the good Father: Meditation on the parable of the prodigal son, sercreyente. com)

as asking him to nurture our hope. Mother Teresa of Calcutta said: "We know that our work is only a drop in the ocean, but that drop, if it were not in the ocean, would disappear, (pray to God to make us generous because He is always generous)."[2] Generosity makes us be safe in God because we are part of that immense sea where hope is not exhausted. We often sense that there is little we can do to remedy suffering, but within us is this vast ocean, we have its vitality.

In Hebrew, "hope" is associated with God, so the term expresses confidence, not in a future outcome, but in the present as a divine force. According to the Psalms, hope is decisive because it comes from God: "My life 'waits' silently for God alone because my hope comes from him. He alone is my rock and my salvation, my fortress; I will not be shaken" (Psalm 62: 5-6). The psalmist is already sure of his liberation since God is the only one in whom he puts his hope.

The Hebrew word for "hope" is the same as for the "gathering" of the waters. The Bible uses the word mikveh when God gathers the waters in creation: "God called the "earth" dry land and the gathering of the waters he called "seas/mikveh" (Genesis 1:10).

Jeremiah relates these gathering waters with hope in God: "Lord, the hope of Israel, everyone who abandons you will be ashamed... because they abandoned the Lord, **the spring of living waters**" (Jeremiah 17:13). Jeremiah's "hope" in God recalls the strength of God as the Creator; just as God gathered (mikveh) the "waters" (mayim) in the past, Jeremiah

---

2   *Verlag, Pattloch, Mother Teresa of Calcutta, A Personal Portrait, Ediciones Palabra, S.A. Madrid. 2012 (Translated from the Spanish).*

describes God as his current "hope" (mikveh) and his "water" (mayim) alive. In biblical language, "hope" is not an abstract desire, but a complete guarantee from God.[3]

Hope is a gift from the Spirit; it gives us confidence in God so we need not fear. In God we find strength, and he enables us to resist temptation. God rejoices when we resist evil. It takes courage to turn to God and admit our need for him. President John F. Kennedy summed it up like this, "Effort and courage are not enough without purpose and direction."[4] Our hope is in God, because we trust in him, and we do not fear.

In God we cannot fear evil because hope arouses strength in us. Three virtues strengthen us: prudence, justice, and temperance. We need these three to grow in a more balanced life.

Jesus said, "of what use is it to man to be generous if he does not share" (cf. Luke 6:38). Jesus says that our love need not have limits because God has given us everything. Jesus invites us to "be merciful as his Father is merciful" (Luke 6:36). And with that he tells us that God's mercy is for everyone. In the parable of the prodigal son, he says it descriptively. The father did not condemn the son who had squandered his fortune. Quite the contrary, he ran to meet him and hugged him. He demanded nothing from him; he welcomed him as his son and celebrated with an extraordinary party saying, "Let's celebrate with a banquet, because this

---

3   *Cf. This is an abstract from Israel Bible Weekly, 'Hope in Hebrew Thought,' by Dr. Nicholas J. Schaser, October 9, 2019.*

4   *Kennedy, John Fitzgerald, El deber y la gloria Testamento político de John F. Kennedy, Editorial Bruguera. 1990 (Spanish).*

son of mine was dead and has come back to life; he was lost, and we have found him." (Luke 15, 23s).

In Greek there are several words for mercy, one of them is *"splanchnizomai"* which means to be moved to the core. The father had empathy for his son because he felt his wounds, he had moved him to the core. I have mentioned this gospel many times and I emphasized how the father felt sorry for his son and did not hesitate to receive him back home.

Jesus is not indifferent to our pain; he is always moved by suffering. If we want to be merciful, we must follow the example in this parable where the father receives his son back by forgiving him. Having mercy implies knowing how to forgive; it means forgiving from the heart without claiming the other. I am merciful when my heart opens to the other because his wounds hurt me. This is the wisdom of the heart --- a merciful heart that gives its life to save another.

This love is within the *circle of life* as the Disney movie "The Lion King" says. As this incredible action of love unfolds, it will unite and unify us in God. That is why we yearn for unity, because deep down in each one of us, we are one, we all belong to each other, because we have the same source of love: God. We are deeply connected in the *circle of life*, beginning with nature and all of creation. We long for life because in the resurrection it is in the essence of our being by the power of Christ. With the resurrection of Jesus, the Holy Spirit initiates a new life, a new *circle of life*. It is the beginning of a new humanity and a new creation where faith and love will find a new place, and blinking the sun enters the sky as the song '*The Circle of Life*' says, when you have time listen to it again:[5]

From the day we arrive on the planet
and, blinking, step into the sun
there's more to see than can ever be seen
more to do than can ever be done
there's far too much to take in here.
More to find than can ever be found
but the sun rolling high
through the sapphire sky.
Keeps great and small on the endless round
it's the circle of life
and it moves us all
through despair and hope
through faith and love
till we find our place
on the path unwinding
in the circle.
The circle of life

If suffering brings us to despair hope in God takes us back to the Circle of Love… God is not indifferent to our suffering, He wants to heal our wounds, especially the wounds of the heart. God is patient and when

---

5   *Song composed by Carmen Twillie and Lebo M. Sung by Elton John in the movie 'The Lion King'.*

we seek him, he will be there to love us and give us his grace. Having lived and suffered, God will want to caress us and assures us that evil will never imprison us.

One of the most beautiful texts that captures the meaning of this new creation is by the mystic Teilhard de Chardin:

> *The day will come when after taking advantage of space, winds, tides and gravity, we will take advantage of the energies of love for God, and that day, for the second time in the history of the world, we will have discovered fire.*[6]

Fire is a powerful symbol of transformation, evoking images of intense heat and binding lightand death and destruction. Where there is fire, there is transforming energy. Saint Elizabeth Ann Seton also speaks of this fire, but for her the fire is Jesus, "Jesus is like a fire in the very center of our soul that always burns. However, we are cold because we do not approach Him." [7]Science can tell us what physical fire is, but religion tells us what spiritual fire does; it forges what exists in its divine identity. The path to this transformation is wisdom, creating windows that open to the depth of the interior, to knowledge from the heart. Wisdom is knowledge deepened by love; it leads us to greater fullness because it sees with the

---

6   Salafranca, Federico Lanzaco, *Apunte para una Espiritualidad Bíblica Universal, Editorial Dei Verbum, S.L. España, 2017*

7   Seton, Elizabeth Bayley. *Collected Writings: Volume 1. New City Press, Hyde Park, New York. 2000.*

inner eye of the heart.

But love goes further because love is the essence of everything that exists. Love makes us see ourselves inside as we are, and for God we are beautiful, you and I live in God, there is no beginning or end, there everything exists in the now, a perpetual present. In that present, we all unite. We need to find love in the center, in ourselves, that depth of love that makes us unique and different, that love centered on God that keeps us united and constantly creates us. To return to us is to live; to return to the interior is to live, rather it is to be fully alive.

Jesus began his public ministry with an invitation to this love, which is why he invites us to conversion "if you make my word your home, you will learn the truth and the truth will set you free" (John 8, 31-32). The reason we are not free is because we are not at home, with ourselves; there is an unsettling urge to become something else, to do something else, to be anywhere other than where we are now, really. Jesus' invitation is, "A new commandment I give you: love one another as I have loved you" (John 13:34).

A new commandment is to learn to think and act in ways that orient us toward the integrated whole of our being. We need to renew our minds and hearts and expand our hearts where life and love are experienced. Love is engraved like fire in the heart. Unless we wake up to this reality, we will continue to block love. Love lives in each of us, the best way to feel it is to get away from the busy world, go into ourselves, appreciate the isolation and return to nature. That is why on Ash Wednesday, when we begin Lent, we are told, *'you are dust and to dust you shall return.'*

When Saint Francis of Assisi heard, *'Go rebuild my church which has fallen into ruin,'* he first took it literally to mean repairing the church where he was praying. So, he collected stones and rebuilt the walls of the church. However, over time he realized that the church cannot be built with stones, but with hearts centered on divine love. So, he gave himself to the project of love, making the love of God the sole purpose of his life. Francisco found Divine love, in the disfigured hand of a leper. Overcoming his revulsion for lepers, he found a God who delights to be among the simple and outcast. Only a heart in love can see God in such circumstances. The revolution of love that Francis started upset many, but it changed the world around him.

Love is not a form of worship; it is a spiritual power that transcends. It is the deepest creative power of human nature. It is to take life as a gift. It responds to the full richness, the variety, the fertility of life itself. This mystery of love we find when internalizing in ourselves, which I spoke of earlier, interior, is something invaluable that American materialism can never understand.

Christianity was never intended to be a religion by the book --- following rules and protocols that would make us holy. In Jesus a new temple of adoration was discovered, the temple of the person, the temple of human love in which God dwells: "Destroy this temple that is made with hands, and in three days I will build another, not made with hands" (Mark 14, 58). What was opened in his life was a new dimension of love, an act of uniting fragmented humanity beyond mere religion.

Being Catholic is doing and acting; it is giving birth, the light of God. Christianity, therefore, must be the love that creates love. "The Word became flesh and dwelt among us" (John 1:40). Life brings together and engages the beauty of life itself, the beauty of love. Christian life arises from union, from love.

The beauty of Saint Francis did not consist of his exterior; his beauty was the interior and radiant goodness of his heart. He arose from a deep encounter with others, especially the rejected ones, even touching the lepers. Francis suffered darkness and experienced many years of doubts, but he persevered in love. Throughout his life, Francis set out to love the poor and those whom society rejected. To love, says Thomas Merton, "You have to leave the cradle where everything is receiving, now you must grow to maturity so that you can give, without worrying about receiving something special in return."[8] Love becomes the luminous presence of God when we renounce the need to control our life and the lives of others, taking away what suffocates life.

Archbishop Oscar Romero also shows that conversion, commitment to life, is only achieved by letting go of the need to control and accept the risk of meeting our fellow men following the example of Christ, Monsignor Romero gave us his life. Risking love can lead us to loneliness because we make ourselves vulnerable, it is the other language of the cross. For Archbishop Romero, this path cost him his life. Also, in El Salvador, it cost the lives of some American Missionaries, two Maryknoll sisters and an Ursuline sister, as well as a lay missionary Jean Donavan who challenged the government for teaching the liberation of the poor in an extremely repressive era. They were all brutally beaten, raped and

---

8   Merton, Thomas. *New Seeds of Contemplation, New Direction Books, New York. 2007.*

murdered. Because of his death, the silence of US collusion was broken, government control was broken, and US support for the Salvadoran government in repressing civil demonstrations was also broken, showing us all what they can achieve. the efforts of a few... voices matter.

I believe we have failed in love and in freedom. The person who gives themself the freedom to be and love without possessing has given meaning to life. On the contrary, those who have lived like this have failed. We fail to get involved and be Christ in the world, a Christ who cares deeply for others. When Archbishop Oscar Romero realized that his friend Father Rutilio Grande had been brutally murdered, fighting for the rights of the poor, he could no longer justify his privileged ecclesiastical life. He identified in solidarity with the poor and became **"the voice of the voiceless,"** giving his life as a "ransom for many." His last sermon before being assassinated speaks to us of the deep inner love that moved him to act. This was part of his last homily...

> *"...The hour has come for the Son of Man to be glorified. Amen, amen, I say to you, unless a grain of wheat falls to the ground and dies, it remains just a grain of wheat; but if it dies, it produces much fruit. Whoever loves his life loses it, and whoever hates his life in this world will preserve it for eternal life. Whoever serves me must follow me, and where I am, there also will my servant be. The Father will honor whoever serves me.[9] You have just heard Christ's Gospel,*

---

9   John 12:23-26

that one must not love oneself so much as to avoid getting involved in the risks of life which history demands of us, that those who would avoid the danger will lose their life, while those who out of love for Christ give themselves to the service of others will live, like the grain of wheat that dies, but only apparently. If it did not die, it would remain alone. The harvest comes about because it dies, allows itself to be sacrificed in the earth and destroyed. This holy Mass is such an act of faith... May this body immolated and this blood sacrifice for humans, feed us so that we can give our body and our blood in suffering and in pain as Christ, not for oneself, but to bring justice and peace to our people."

Through his suffering on the cross, Christ unites us in one body, on one cross where we find the love that is the basis of our faith. The cross is not simply the passion of Christ; it is also the passion of God. This embrace of the crucified Christ is what the Eucharist means. In the "Eucharist," we celebrate the divine love that begins in us. However, it is not simply an expression, it is an empowerment through which the Eucharist in each person receives the complete Christ, head and members, so the whole body is present in each member, knowing Christ now means that our relationship with Christ must already be, a relationship between us and with all creation.

If we say yes to the embrace of Christ crucified, then we must offer that embrace to others. Eucharist means being internally related to others in love; it is the source of a holistic-Catholic personality and the emergence of a new humanity united by love. Every day, in some way, we are challenged to become the bread that is broken for the hungry.

The Eucharist is a self-definition of relationship that transforms strangers into family. It is a sacrament that should promote new patterns of relationship. Through baptism, we are immersed in the life of God and immersed in the whole event of Christ; we live and will rise with Him. It is the good news of our liberation. In the Eucharist, we commit ourselves to the beginning of a new future. Those who participate in the Eucharist are asked to "remember" being members of that death and resurrection of Jesus, not as a past event but as the power of the future. A Eucharistic community is a new energy field through which relationships generate new patterns of love, mercy, compassion, and forgiveness. Each Eucharistic celebration marks the beginning of a new future. As sacraments, baptism and the Eucharist are public commitments and expressions of Christian love that generate more love, more being, and more awareness. The Eucharist sanctifies us.

In the death and resurrection of Jesus, we have new life. What happened in Jesus is a foretaste of humanity's future, a radical transformation through the power of God's life-giving spirit. Saint Bonaventure says: "It is said that all things are transformed in the transfiguration of Christ to the extent that something of each creature was transfigured into Christ. For us human beings, Christ has something in common with all creatures and all of creation. With the stone, He shares existence; with animals, He shares sensations; and with the angels, he shares intelligence. Thus, all things are transformed into Christ, since in his human nature he embraced something of each creature to himself when he was transfigured."[10] In Jesus, God comes as the future; we see in the life of Jesus the creative power of love and the promise of a new life.

The world is a community of love in which one's own identity is found in each other. When we die, we enter the process of falling in love. The Christian, through the power of love, enters a communion with God, through the incarnation of Jesus. The Christian enters the divine mystery where humanity is in transformation and perfection. We must perfect ourselves in God because we are connected to Him through love and in tune with creation in the light of the Spirit.

Jesus is born through the community and participates in its creation. Therefore, this important aspect in the divine incarnation must be reproduced in each one of us. In this we live spontaneous, creative, provocative love that inflames the heart.

Life is an indefinite process until we reach perfection in love. That is why the human being is called to be part of the whole --- not only of the world but of the entire universe. The physical structure of the universe is love. We are part of that love, that universe. That is why the Christian life is not about laws, authority and power. It is about love, and it seeks to find love in the hearts of others. To better understand what I am sharing, one needs to be conscious of the Mystery dwelling within each of us. Our challenge is to maintain love in a world that resists and fears being rejected. Love empowers us to go beyond ourselves and to create a world of love.

---

10   Buenaventura, San. *Itinerario de la Mente de Dios. Editorial Claretiana. España, 1990 (Translated from the English).*

The scientist Albert Einstein, known worldwide for the development of the Theory of Relativity and who revolutionized known science until the 20th century, said two things that impressed me:

The most beautiful thing we can experience is the mysterious. It is the source of all true art and all science. He to whom this 'emotion' is a stranger, who can no longer pause to wonder, or stand rapt in awe, is as good as death. His eyes are closed. Knowing that what is impenetrable to us really exists, manifesting itself as the maximum prudence and the most radiant beauty. That our clumsy capacities can understand only in its most primitive forms... This knowledge, this feeling, is at the core of religious truth. In that sense, and in that sense only, I belong to the ranks of devout religious men.

The idea that this universe in all its millionfold order and precision is the result of blind chance is a credible as the idea that if a printshop blew up all the type would fall down again in the finished and faultless form of the dictionary. There is only two ways to live your life. One is as though nothing is a miracle.

97

The other is as though everything is a miracle.[11]

This mystery gains more strength when lived in the cross of Christ. United with Christ is that we understand the true source of truth. This mystery encloses all of creation: the earth, all peoples, other religions, animals and all living beings. For this we must forge new relationships of love that include all creation: the earth, all peoples, other religions, animals, and all living things. We need to reinvent ourselves in love, realizing that, on the timeline, Christianity is born this morning and is awakening to the novelty of new life. In Jesus, divine love erupted with hope and dreams for a new world. This new world is within our reach if we awaken to the power of inner love to create anew.

We can only awaken to the power of love to create this new world by dying to our earthly one. The best gift that life gives us is death because that is where we are truly born to love. But the vast majority of people fear death; it is an unknown entity. It would be easier to remain in the world --- a world we already learned to deal with. American film director, actor, and comedian Woody Allen jokingly commented one day, "I am not afraid of death; I just don't want to be there when it happens." Leaving our present life is not fearful if we first fall in love with God and open our hearts to him. Death is then part of life and must be expected as a reward, as a gift from God. So, let's wait for death with joy.

I experienced death when I entered religious life. I was 19 years old.

---

11   Calaprice, Alice. *The Ultimate Quotable Einstein (On religion, God, and philosophy / Attributed to Einstein). Princeton University Press and the Hebrew University of Jerusalem. New Jersey, 2011, Pgs. 331 & 483.*

I say I experienced death because I died to myself to be born again. Most recently when I entered the hospital with the COVID virus. When I felt the proximity of death, I sent a text message to Mario Rodríguez, whom I have mentioned before, to tell him the fallowing.

> *They're going to prepare me*
> *I don't know what the Lord wants.*
> *I already abandoned myself to Him.*
> *I've not getting better. Yesterday I confessed*
> *and I received Jesus --- I'm ready.*[12]

I was prepared to face death because of what I had learned in the Spirituality of the Cross, which the Missionaries of the Holy Spirit embrace. This spirituality taught me that pain and suffering can transform us if they are offered and united with the sufferings of Christ. We are called to experience pain and suffering to transform it into salvation. This mystery of the cross is experienced in solitude "...My God, my God, why have you forsaken me?" (Matthew 27, 46).

Before we can become effective instruments of salvation for ourselves and others, we must love as Jesus loves, and accept suffering as Jesus accepted it. Let us remember that most of our years on this earth will suffer as in a 'valley of tears'. God speaks to us with great sweetness when He invites us to suffer, which is only reduced to making a change of life.

---

12   *I wrote this text to Mario Rodríguez at 10:35 a.m., Saturday, September 19, 2020.*

We must ask God for the strength.

Cardinal John Henry Newman said, "To live is to change, and to be perfect is to change a lot."[13] That insight from Newman is comforting. It is also clear that we learn more from our failures than from our achievements, and that is where spiritual courage enlightens us through change. For in the spiritual life suffering is not avoided, on the contrary, it is fully opened to it, not only ours but everyone's. There in the very entrails of the other we feel the pain already the pain of both of us... this requires courage and honesty; is what I understand when we say **Jesus' savior of all people...** **SAVE THEM.** Here the path becomes a sacrament of hope. There we find freedom, there life is in tune with the present. Love helps us to accept the grace of change and become a sanctuary for ourselves.

I experienced a life change when I got sick; there I immersed myself in love. I was aware of my situation and that I would not return to this life. I spoke with God and put myself totally in his hands as I crossed the threshold of death. It was three months in a coma, plus another month in delicate treatment in which, already conscious, I suffered unspeakable things, you can already imagine, permanent syringes, endless interference by the medical team when what I wanted was simply to rest, and last more than a month in recovery (more than five months in total). God allowed me to know and experience love.

After my time in the hospital, I spent over a month in a recovery center (Marysville) and then in my community in Banks, Oregon. I have

---

13   Newman, John Henry. *Sermones Católicos. Ediciones Rialp, Madrid, 2016* (*translated from the Spanish*).

spent those days and months recovering. This time has been a blessing because I have understood how fragile and short life can be and how little control, we humans have. We desperately need God; so we need not to worry about sickness and suffering.

When I got to the hospital,[14] I thought I would be there for a short time, but I soon realized that I wasn't. I had to be transferred by helicopter to another hospital because that hospital center had the appropriate technology to treat me, this hospital was in another city. They had to decide between the option of sending me in an ambulance, but given my seriousness, they did not guarantee that I would arrive alive, so they changed to send me by helicopter. It was a very rainy day with strong winds that did not allow the helicopter to take off in the usual way; faced with this dilemma and after evaluating the situation, they authorized, given the gravity, to send me by helicopter because otherwise, I would not arrive alive. Luckily, I did not know that they transferred me, despite the storm, because had I known it would have been nervous.

I thought I would be there a short time, but I soon learned that would not be the case. I had to be transferred in an emergency by helicopter to another hospital in the city. It was a rainy day with strong winds, which did not allow the helicopter to land in the usual manner. Luckily, I was unaware that they transferred me precariously, despite the storm, to the

---

14   *I first arrived at Providence St. Vincent Medical Center; from there I was rushed to Providence Portland Medical Center.*

ICU. I arrived to be connected to ECMO,[15] as my lungs had failed by then.

The medical staff gave my family little hope that I would still be alive, a decision had to be made to keep me alive by machines or take me offline to prevent me from suffering. But my brother priests, my family and so many others continued to pray for a miracle. God works differently.

During these months, they assured that I would die. After more than two months on the threshold of death, two of my sisters, Lidia and Alicia, along with my niece Adriana, noticed that I moved my left leg. When informing the nurse I had moved my leg, she in response immediately assured that it was a reflex and that the body did it unintentionally. But when they communicated this news to the rest of my family, my brother priest in the province and friends, there was great hope in them and prayer intensified.

Life surged again in my dying body. The frequent dialysis and my dependency on ECMO gradually decreased as my organs began to function independently, but it left me with serious consequences; in fact,

---

15   *The Extracorporeal Membrane Oxygenation system or ECMO, is a mechanical ventilation equipment that allows the respiratory function to perform and clean the blood, while the lungs can remain less active. Specifically, ECMO is considered a rescue technique for patients with respiratory failure secondary to certain diseases. These are cases in which not enough oxygen reaches the blood and the necessary carbon dioxide is not expelled, or even both situations. In these circumstances, the use of ECMO may be considered if other mechanical ventilation tools or conventional methods are not working. The operation of ECMO consists of extracting blood from a patient's vein, with the help of a specific cannula or tube. Then, it goes to an artificial circuit, which is external to the body, for oxygenation and cleaning (a centrifugal pump transports the blood to an oxygenator, where oxygen is supplied and excess CO2 is eliminated. It should be added that it is possible to use ECMO for days or weeks at a time, but once the patient is stabilized, the standard method of mechanical ventilation is used.*

I still have shortness of breath and I get tired very easily. It is a challenge for me to get back to my previous level of health and energy. The process I am going through requires a lot of patience and humility; now I am very vulnerable, I will clarify this statement in a chapter.

They gave me my life back. Now I know what gift that is. My recovery will continue for a long time, although my body is working surprisingly well. The doctors could not believe that such a recovery was possible since they assumed that when I disconnected, I would die, when they admitted me, the diagnosis was that if I survived, I would spend the rest of my life under constant dialysis. From that time, the entire medical staff was ready to disconnect me. You will ask how I felt when I woke up from the coma?

My sister-in-law Albina was with me when I woke up, more than three months had passed. I called her name and she was surprised. 'Do you know me?' and she asked me to repeat her name and I said: "Why?" The doctors had told the family that when if I woke up, I would not recognize anyone. 'Do you know my husband?' 'Arturo!' I replied. Hearing my answer, she cried. It was evident that my brain was working. Two nurses came in and, surprised, one of them exclaimed, '*Thanks be to God, thanks be to God.*' What followed was tests carried out by several doctors. They couldn't believe what was happening. He had come back to life. Today I am still in recovery and I am learning to offer all my aftereffects with sacrifice. Love opens us to the acceptance of suffering.

I am called to be an instrument of God and lead others to salvation and an intimate relationship with God. God exists, and he is with us daily, holding us close to him like a father lovingly embracing his child. His love is unconditional and always present. Let us be an example to others when we are in the midst of suffering and pain, and let that suffering transform us and lead us to the heart of Christ. Let's say to God like the psalm, 'Teach us to number our days, so that wisdom may enter our hearts' (Psalm 90, 12).

Each person, each part of creation, is an aspect of God's self-expression because we are close to Him. I came back to life because God allowed me to, knowing the consequence of the trauma I would experience. That is why I want to share my experience in this book and continue trusting God with love.

I have never felt better as a priest than I am right now after COVID and hospitalization. My life on this earth was almost over and I know that the extra time I have been given should be better spent. I want prayer to have a special place in my life and in my priestly ministry like never before. The priest must be a witness of God, a witness of his love. I must be zealous in preaching the word of God to bring people to realize God's love for them. Our example is what will draw people to the Lord.

I accepted God's call to be a priest and live in a community of religious, The Congregation of the Missionaries of the Holy Spirit (MSpS). I did not imagine the way of life I would live, nor the number of people I would meet and bring closer to God. It has been a beautiful and challenging life. My priestly ministry has helped countless people throughout my 22 years as a priest. I have confessed to countless people, I have kept many confessions in my heart because they have transformed me and I have come closer to God, they have been life-giving because I have risen with confidence to continue interceding for others and when I have experienced desolation.

The priest, by his ministry (sacraments) and prayer, is an intercessor of the merciful love of God. Also, through the proclaimed Word, he intercedes in mercy. People see God in the priest... and really the priest must be a perfect intercessor between God and men.

In my experience, this has been a blessing, but it has also been overwhelming. I have little experience and sadly, I have made many people feel bad who came to trust me and I feel sorry for disappointing them. One person who experienced great disappointment with me even threatened me with death. During those days, it was difficult to reconcile my sleep. You may wonder what I did to him to make him feel this way, I simply told him that his wife couldn't sing (they were both in the choir and his wife insisted on singing the responsorial psalm).

My priestly hands have blessed many people, I have blessed objects (many religious), houses, businesses, cars, boats, motorcycles, bicycles and many animals... I have given myself to God body and soul, but I have also given myself as an object because that is how I have felt when people keep asking me for favors. And it is my hand they usually use to take advantage of me... My consecrated hand gives God's blessing.

I want to invite you to put your lives in God's hands. I know that suffering produces fear, but the grace of God helps us overcome that fear. God promises us his Spirit to bravely face suffering. That special gift of the Spirit is peace and strength to help us face illness and the most difficult times that pain can bring. We can only appreciate and patiently endure suffering helped by God. We will often experience pain in our lives; That is when we need to turn to the Lord and trust him to give us the help we need.

Because of my weakness, after the hospitalization, I did not have the desire to do anything, but the Lord strengthened me when I prayed to Him. Let us remember that the Lord invites us; "Come to me, all you who are weary and burdened, and I will give you rest. Take my yoke upon you and learn from me, for I am meek and humble of heart, and you will find rest for your soul because my yoke is easy and My burden is light" (Matthew 11: 28-30). Jesus says his yoke will be light on our shoulders, but it can be quite heavy. Jesus says it is possible to bear our burdens because the yoke is attached, like it is to a pair of oxen, with Jesus bearing the weight with us.

Thus, the yoke and the cross fall on our shoulders through suffering and pain. That is how it was for me when I was ill; the cross became my constant companion, a reminder of my own death. The cross always accompanies us. When you feel troubled and the cross feels heavy, I invite you to pray this prayer of Saint Francis:

Lord, make me an instrument of your peace.
Where there is hatred, let me carry love.
Where there is offense, let me carry forgiveness.
Wherever there is discord, may the union lead me.
Where there is doubt, let me carry faith.
Where there is error, let me carry truth.
Where there is despair, may I carry joy.
Where there is darkness, let me carry Light.
Oh, Master, make me seek not so much to be consoled,
but to console; to be understood, but to understand;
to be loved, as to love.
Because it is in giving that we receive;

forgiving, that one is forgiven;
and in dying, that we are resurrected
to Eternal Life.[16]

Carrying the cross will be easy when Jesus carries it with us and at times even for us. Saint Paul affirms this: "Who will separate us from the love of Christ? Trials, affliction, persecution, hunger, danger, or the sword? As the scripture says: Because of you they continually drag us to death, they treat us like sheep destined for slaughter. But no, in all that we will be successful thanks to the One who loved us. I know that neither death nor life, neither angels nor the forces of the universe, neither the present nor the future, nor the spiritual forces, whether from heaven or the abyss, nor any other creature will be able to separate us from the love of God, manifested in Christ Jesus our Lord" (Rom, 8, 35-39).

The victory over this life opens the way for us to eternal life with Christ: "Where, oh death is your victory? Where, O death, is your sting? The sting of death is sin, and the law made it more powerful. But we thank God who gives us the victory through Jesus Christ our Lord. So, my dearly beloved brothers, stand firm and do not be moved. Dedicate yourselves to the Lord's work at all times, aware that with Him your work will not be sterile" (1 Corinthians 15, 55-58).

The cross is linked to loneliness, but not to sadness; we cannot be sad if we love God and work for his kingdom. Mother Teresa of Calcutta lived

---

16   Pombo, Álvaro. *Vida de San Francisco de Asís, Editorial Grupo Planeta,*
España, 2011.

many years in solitude, but she always kept a smile because she dedicated herself to the Lord's work. She said, "A smile is the beginning of love. Be kind and merciful. Make whoever approaches you feel good and feel happy." [17]Thomas Merton said, "Love can only be preserved when it is gifted with a smile."[18] One psalm says, "Turn away from evil and do good, seek peace and follow it with a smile" (Psalm 34, 13).

We make peace when we seek peace and work for peace with a smile. The smile brings joy and joy brings peace, that is its language. The word "joy" comes from the Latin "gaudere": to rejoice. When I rejoice, my heart leaps for joy. Joy is linked to the joy of living, a feeling that comes from the heart. The word "pleasure" is also derived from the Latin "voluptatem". The joy and pleasure of living makes the heart jump with joy. The most intense joy is experienced by those who put virtues into practice. It is an energy that stimulates and awakens life. Joy is a healing and stimulating force that generates vitality and prompts action. Emotions can be linked to joy, especially when they mobilize us to act. The term emotion comes from moving. There are thousands of little joys we each experience throughout the day. When we experience these joys, we feel deep happiness and we feel empowered. That is why Jesus communicates eternal life and life in abundance. Eternal life is not after death; it is now, that is why it is stronger than death.

---

17   *The Joy of Loving, Mather Theresa. Compile by Yaya, Chalica, Pinguin Book, 1997*

18   *Merton, Thomas. New Seeds of Contemplation, New Direction Books, New York. 2007.*

In Jesus, there is life in abundance; whoever participates in the life of God lives forever. The life lived now in time is temporary. Abundance (or fullness) also means overflowing and there, too, faith grows. That is why thinking about death now is thinking about this non-temporal life. Death is a step to prepare for it. In the Gospel of John, Jesus says of himself, "I came that they might have life and have it more abundantly." (John 10, 10). Saint Augustine says that joy brings us to the depths of our soul. It puts us in contact with our soul, and that joy is the source of life. Only those who rejoice can live their faith completely. Meister Eckhart puts it this way: "God is the newest thing there is, the youngest thing, and if we are united to God, we become new again, and thus rejoice."[19] If our hearts are open to Christ, then we are changing because we are always born anew in Christ. How God proposes that rebirth in Christ, the psalm says: "Sing to the Lord a new song." (Psalm 8, 35). The joy of the heart is only enjoyed if you live with others; that is why the Bible says that it is not good for man to be alone (cf., Genesis 2,18). Life always happens in relationship.

Saint Augustine says, "He who sings praises not only praises, but also praises with joy."[20] Let us praise God, the source of blessings, with joy. Let's sing because we love the Lord. The soul feeds on what delights it and often what delights it is to sing with feeling to seal it with the heart. The

---

19   *Meditations with Eckhart, into. And trans Matthew Fox (Sant Fe, NM: Bear and Company, 1983), 32*

20   *Hipona, Agustin. Meditaciones de San Agustin. Editorial Ivory Falls Books, 2018. New York (Translated from the Spanish).*

feelings bring hope; if I have feelings of happiness, then surely, I will smile and be thankful to be alive.

Mahatma Gandhi put it like this, "Happiness is when what you think, what you say and what you do are in harmony."[21] Consider these three biblical texts for your reference:

1. A joyful heart is the health of the body (Proverbs 17, 22).

2. A tranquil mind gives life to the body, but jealousy rots the bones. Those who oppress the poor revile their Maker, but those who are kind to the needy honor him" (Ecclesiastes 14, 30-31).

3. Remember your Creator in the days of your youth, before the evil days come and the years approach of which you will say, "I have no pleasure in them" (Ecclesiastes 12:1).

These texts tell us you don't need any special reason to rejoice. Live life simply; then, you will find sufficient reasons to delight yourself.

The church fathers believe that delight in God is a joy that will always be with us. It cannot be taken away from us even by painful experiences because God never departs from us. In each of us, there is a source of joy. But that joy is often dry because it is based on the material. The good news of the gospel is that it wants to put us in touch with this source. Spirituality consists of putting the person in contact with his essence. The deepest vocation of the human being is joy; nothing blocks happiness.

Joy gives us strength, freshness and vitality. A fountain must flow, it is a sign it has water. Psychology speaks of "feelings of flow." We need our lives to flow and see that the source of our lives is a blessing. We have been

---

21   *Deshpande, M. S., Pathway to God, Navajivan Publishing House, 1971. India.*

sent to this world to fulfill a mission. The original mission that God gave to Adam and Eve was: "Be fruitful and multiply" (Genesis 1, 28). This does not necessarily mean having children, but life must be fruitful, so we cannot be sad. Our task then will be to rejoice and be a blessing to others. Each of us must fulfill this mission in a personal way. Each one should be a blessing to the others, and then it will be a world of happiness. Some are a blessing by their very existence and/or by their personal radiance; About this, I want to share with you something that, although it seemed trivial at the time, had great significance for me. When I lived in California, I visited Disneyland and I liked it a lot, but what struck me the most was seeing the joy of the people; I never met someone angry. I enjoyed it so much I took out a membership so I could go as often as possible; I went over three times a month.

Each of us has his own personal gifts, charisms; you too. Each can be a light to illuminate the darkness of the other and of a world that has forgotten goodness and light. You and I meet people daily and leave an impression, a personal touch or a gift, a mark of life. Decide to "leave your mark" to influence others for good; this will change our world person by person.

One more thing about joy: it is good for mental and spiritual health. Those who make others laugh win heaven. We can all make others happy; we do a lot of good when we provoke a smile. Let us listen to God to cheer up those who are sad and rejoice with them. Let's make joy a reality that speaks of hope. Remember that hope is like the sun, if you only believe in it when you see it, you will never get over the night. We will overcome the night and the darkness with the sun that is Christ Jesus.

Let us enlighten those who need the light to clear the path of salvation. We can because we belong to love. We can because we are children of God. We can because we live happily.

Find Calm
through Meditation

The pandemic brought anguish, many mornings are now sad, and the days and weeks are lived with uncertainty. It is definitely a nightmare or perhaps a misfortune. But what is COVID -19? It is a disease? Yes… COVID is a disease that is triggered in the respiratory tract and seriously affects them (the upper respiratory tract: paranasal sinuses, nose and throat, and the lower trachea and lungs). It spreads through person-to-person contact and on surfaces where the virus is found.

How long will it last? Hopefully, it will soon be part of history and read only in textbooks. Today it continues and many continue to die while others suffer the consequences of being infected, such is my case. The effects and consequences are many, those of us who suffer it know it from experience. Unfortunately, many refuse to be vaccinated. There are theories that everything was planned by outside interests to harm humanity. All these theories hit hard on the head of many stubborn people and they are easily convinced. As soon as the vaccines were available, I took advantage of them, I already have the first two vaccines and the third (the one they call a booster).

There are many people against vaccines. They say that the ingredients in them are highly dangerous and can alter DNA. They say they deposit a microchip in the vaccine to activate it later and control your life. Ask yourself, who are these people and what do they really want? I invite you to become aware of what you have experienced and discern what is best for you. Our physical and mental health was greatly affected, so now let God enter your life and with Him and in Him discern the best, but in prayer.

I want to conclude with seven meditations --- We have spent a lot of time worrying, some got sick and many died. We have mourned their absence. Now we need time for ourselves, to live and enjoy life. I invite you to listen to this song:[1]

Don't worry about a thing
Every little thing is gonna be alright
Rise up this morning
Smiled with the rising sun
Three little birds
By my doorstep
Singin' sweet songs
Of melodies pure and true
This is my message to you.
Don't worry about a thing
Every little thing is gonna be alright.

---

1   *Three Little Birds / Bob Marley and the Wailers. Released as a single in 1980. It is one of Marley's most popular songs and has been covered by numerous other artists. The song is often thought to be named "Don't Worry About a Thing" or "Every Little Thing is Gonna Be All Right."*

Rise up this morning'
Smiled with the rising' sun
Three little birds
By my doorstep
Singin' sweet songs
Of melodies pure and true
This is my message to you.

First Meditation

Enter your inner peace. You need to unplug and go back to your inner music, your sexuality that defines who you are, the one that leads you to experience joy and sadness. Listen to your body and mind. Listen also to your physical and mental experiences. In I Corinthians (12, 12-27) Paul mentions that our body has many parts and each part has many purposes... Paul concludes by saying that all these parts must be united to Christ. Is this the time to join Christ?

Do the following: listen to your favorite music, the one that calms you and breathe while you ask God to give you peace.

Every day our body feels different, every day is also different, creation changes every day. If our body feels different every day, shouldn't you consider listening to it, what does it tell you? What does your body need today? My recovery has challenged me and my physical therapist now recommends a simple exercise, inhaling and exhaling throughout the day. Your mind may be absent because you pay more attention to the cell phone, television or computer. You need to become more aware of your surroundings, the beauty of nature, the changing landscapes. Leave the less important things and do something different that relaxes you.

COVID brought me to mindfulness. Each morning I enjoy my coffee and that coffee gives me the energy to begin the new day as I taste that sip of energy and caffeine. I thank God for the gift of being alive. Never before was I aware of the food that goes into my mouth and down to my stomach unless I happened to be in a restaurant or at an event where the food was described previously by the waitress or the menu. Now I focus on what I chew, and I use all my senses, especially my salivary glands, even for a tiny bite, or one slow sip of coffee as I deeply inhale the rich aroma. I invite you not to eat so fast, enjoy each bite, distinguish the flavors and mention them out loud so you can remember them later. It is a simple exercise and it makes you aware that life has flavor... and it often comes through the mouth.

Saint Francis de Sales, in his book, 'The Devout Life' invites us to prepare the day with the following practice:

In the morning, prepare your soul to be at peace. Take care throughout the day to remember that resolution and to reaffirm it. Should you become disturbed, do not lose heart and do not be pained by it, but having recognized the situation calmly humble yourself before God and attempt to restore your mind to peace. Say to your soul: "Now, friend, we have made a misstep, let us proceed more carefully." And each time you fall, do the same thing. When you are at peace, make good use of the time, making as many acts of humility as you can, however insignificant they may be. For as our Lord says, he who is faithful in little things will have great ones entrusted to him. Above all, do no lose your courage, but be patient, watchful, and ready with a spirit of compassion. God will hold you in his hand, and if he lets you stumble, it will be only so thar you realize that you would collapse entirely if he did not hold you, and thus to make you tighten your grip upon his hand.[1]

---

1   Armida, Concepción Cabrera. *Roses Among Thorns*. Christopher O. Blum, *Sophia Institute Press. Manchester, NH. 2014*

Second Meditation

Whenyou get out of bed, sit down for 2 minutes and thank
God for the beginning of a new day, think about the things you will do
and breathe slowly. When brushing your teeth, do it slowly --- rinse your
mouth and thank God for the water that is refreshing your mouth, at the
end, breathe consciously (inhale and exhale).

Then focus your attention on the positives of the day as you step
into the shower. Feel the warm water embracing your body. As you bathe,
thank God for the luxury of clean water that refreshes you and wakes you
up completely. Keep God present while you wash. If you bathe with soap
or shampoo, realize that many people are denied this gift, even the water
itself.

Let the water run down your body and think about the areas of your
life you could improve, kindness towards others? Patience? Generosity?
Ask God to help you be better. Wash yourself thinking you eliminate all
the bad while you clean your body, if you have sinned, let the soap clean
you and symbolically renew you.

After four months in the hospital in Marysville, I had my first
bath. It was very refreshing. I felt so alive, the water reminded me of my
baptism and at that moment, I smiled with joy. The nurse who bathed me
noticed my smile and asked if I was happy. *Yes, the water reminded me of*

my baptism, I feel that with this bath, I was reborn, I replied.

God has made us wonderfully; bathing is always pleasing, bathing gives me joy, it puts me in a good mood, this is vital for life. There is a connection with our emotional health and physical health. Those with a cheerful and positive outlook are much more likely to have better physical health. Those who rarely laugh or spend long periods in overly serious states are less able to handle the stress of illness and illness itself.

When you bathe, I invite you to enjoy the water, to feel the water like living water that refreshes and renews you.

One of my nieces usually pampers me by sending me soap and shampoo; being in Marysville, I received that gift. I smiled with joy and the nurse who bathed me liked the smell so much she asked me to tell my niece where she had bought it, she wanted to know this so she could buy it.

Third Meditation

How to live with equanimity, or how to be more equanimous? First, know that we all have a purpose in life. God has aligned it for us in daily choices, this purpose has great meaning and harmonizes with energy so you can carry out all your actions with joy.

I invite you to do the following: any time during the week take time to close your eyes and settle your mind and body, and see yourself as the beloved daughter/son whom God loves and is well pleased (see Matthew 3:17). Now, answer each question:

Are you serving others?
How do you serve?
What matters most to you?
Why?

There is always a purpose in life, finding its meaning will connect you to everything and harmonize you with your virtues and gifts from God. Recognize your gifts, in a quiet time, breathe deeply and thank God for each one of them. Say slowly, I use this gift (mention the first gift) for this… continue the phrase.

Many situations can change our emotions and if they are out of control these can interrupt our days, weeks and months… and yes, sadly, our years. We need to admit that such frustrations take us to anger and fear. This can block our peace and joy, and it can affect our health and our relationships. If we suppress these feelings, we end up in insolation, we need to relate with our emotions. I want to say it as "dating our emotions."

May I recommend: Don't be afraid to name your emotions. Feel them, bring them to caress your body by directing your attention to the emotion. Bring empathy by looking at each side of the emotion. By becoming aware of it you will learn what is going on in your head and that will help you to balance the three areas that are conversing: feelings, head and heart.

Now do the following: hug yourself with compassion, not reasoning. It is much easier to self-criticize your actions and this will always lead to self-esteem. A compassionate God has the tools to deal with your setbacks. You must remember that God is love and God LOVES YOU. Every day remember the phrase I shared with you earlier...

God loves me and
is pleased with me.

As you say it, put your right hand on your heart, breathe slowly and deeply and repeat it as many times as you want…

Lord my heart is yours

122

and I love you.

After the hospitalization and the time in Marysville, I would take a walk, taking advantage of this time to meditate. We all need this regularly, an antidote to the frenetic pace we live in these days. I invite you to walk, this should not take much effort; walking makes us aware of the ground that is there supporting us. Walk at the pace that is most comfortable for you, but focus on each of your movements, step by step; try to coordinate them with your breathing.

I would invite Mary, mother of God, to walk with me and usually say a few prayers while talking to her. If you walk, I invite you to the following: find a quiet place to walk, where you will not be distracted or interrupted by acquaintances. Walk and inhale with awareness, think of God and think once again that God loves you, that you are very special to Him and that He created this world for you and the environment you see while you walk is yours, take advantage of this time of union with God to feel it is your time and no one else's.

Fourth Meditation

We are a beautiful creation of God, each of us is unique, there is no replica of us, we have our own DNA. Meister Eckhart writes: "There is something in the soul that is so like God that we are one with Him."[1] Our creativity comes from God, so God is creative in us. It is God's creation --- Do you share your creativity? I invite you to be creative, share your creativity with others, make others join you in what you are creating, be it painting, preparing food, etc.

In God, we have a place in creation since Divine love is expressed in us so that we can create. Therefore, the term creation points to what is always becoming: love. Without us humans, creation lacks what it still needs to be complete. Creation is not so much an event in the past. God does not exist apart from his creation. Creation is an integral part of God's very nature. God is eternally committed to her. Divine transcendence is the faculty of love where the being desires more and love seeks more love. Get used to being connected with nature, with your five sounds. Do not be distracted by the buzz of the city, what matters are the melodies of the world, the song of the birds. Open your ears and your heart to feel

---

1   *Meditations with Eckhart, into. And trans Matthew Fox, Sant Fe, NM: Bear and Company, 1983*

connected on a deep level. Inhale and breathe deeply, become aware that with every breath, God is present in you, try to feel the temperature of the air, no matter if it's cold or hot, God will be there with you.

Look for ways to add warmth or cheer to your days... cultivate warmth, intimacy, and connection. Remember that it will also boost your spirit and increase your well-being year-round. Consider the following:

- Create comfortable and pleasant lighting. Light candles at night, do not wait for a special event. Light a fire (if you have a fireplace, it would be the best); the flames attract people and there, you can create connection.
- Enjoy a hot chocolate or tea after a busy day. Play games to promote joy and camaraderie. Read a favorite story or novel.
- Cook food that makes you feel comfortable. Certain foods are associated with comfort, especially homemade ones (beef broth, chicken or meatballs). Plan dinner parties sure to send comforting aromas from the kitchen.

Fifth Meditation

When this pandemic is over, you can say hello and hug. Don't be afraid to hug everyone and everything, even trees. My first community walk was to the beach in Oregon, but before arriving we stopped for a while in a beautiful park to appreciate the huge trees (a common thing in Oregon). I separated myself from Mario and Juan José for a moment to privately contemplate a beautiful tree I saw in the distance and I felt the need to be close to it, to feel its bark, to hug it; I even thought of talking to him and told him I wish he could share his vitality and strength with me. I was able to feel its coolness and smell its dew as I hugged it; this action gave me a very pleasant and rewarding experience.

Having hugged the tree, it seems that they caused its roots to become jealous, because when I tried to return to my brothers, the roots caught me and I fell hard to the ground, I scratched my face, I did not know, but the fall was so strong that I bled. I wanted to get up, but I couldn't, it was difficult for me to get up, but thank God my brothers came to help me up. They asked me what had happened. Mario burst out laughing when he heard my response, "I just wanted to hug that tree." While Juan José kept at a distance.

Every time I am near a tree, I am reminded of a book I read some time ago and I really liked it, it is called, *"The Giving Tree"* by Shel Silvertein.[1] The book shares the life of an apple tree and a boy, who developed a relationship. The tree is very generous to the boy as he grows into a teenager, an adult, and finally an old man. Even though the boy grows, the tree always addresses him as "Boy." As a child, the Boy plays with the tree, climbs it, swings on its branches, and eats its apples. With passing time, he visits him less, and when he does visit the tree it's only to take something from it. To make him happy, the tree ended up being just a trunk… hence the name of the book, The Generous Tree.

The love of the tree was the same through the years, but that of the 'Child' was of interest and sometimes of disinterest, perhaps frivolous. This book talks about love through time and space. I share with you part of the conclusion of the book, hoping that when you can give yourself the time to read it one day, it is really short:

After a long time, they boy came back again.

- "I am sorry, Boy," said the tree, "but I have nothing left to give you, my apples are gone."

- "My teeth are too weak for apples," said the boy.

- "My branches are gone," said the tree.

"You cannot swing them,"

- "I am too old to swing on branches," said the boy.

- "My trunk is gone," said the tree.

- "You cannot climb," "I am to tire to climb," said the boy.

---

1   Silvertein, Shel. The Giving Tree, Harper Colling Publishers. 1964. China.

- "I am sorry," signed the tree. "I wish that I could give you something... but I have nothing left. I am just an old stump.

- I am sorry... "I don't need very much now," said the boy, "just a quiet place to sit and rest. I am very tired."

- "Well," said the tree, straightening herself up as much as she could,

- "on old stump is good for sitting and resting.

- Come, Boy, sit down. Sit down and rest."

Sixth Meditation

When you greet someone, greet them with enthusiasm, get excited because you can still greet someone, get excited because you can still greet someone, and if you usually say 'I love you' or say 'I love you' don't be afraid to look this person in the eye. In our society, many people feel isolated (of course, with the pandemic this is now very common). In the church, after mass, people usually greet the priest at the end of mass; some parishioners usually want to shake hands goodbye and some others like to say goodbye with a hug.

Due to the epidemic, we were recommended not to wave and hug. For me, this was difficult, I cannot deprive myself of giving a hug. During my 21 years as a priest, I have learned there are people who need a hug. I remember that, once during the rite of reconciliation, a young man of approximately 23 years old confessed; after listening to him and receiving absolution, I thought this young man needed a hug; I asked him if I could hug him and he accepted immediately. I left the confessional to hug him and when he felt my sincerity and affection, he slowly let go of tears, I thought this gesture had been enough, but I soon realized this young man refused to let go of me; After long minutes, he told me he had never received a hug, I told him, 'I give you this hug and God also gives it to you' Since that day I cannot refuse to give a hug, so I usually accept them when

129

given the occasion. To end this book, I simply want to say: smile, wave, hug, and love your neighbor as yourself.

Deliberately, without succumbing to your own reactions and judgments, embrace yourself, love yourself. For example, you could start by treating yourself to a massage. This is an act of kindness that will soften your soul and your relationships, especially if you are overwhelmed by conflicts. If a massage is not to your liking, then take 45 minutes or an hour to take a good bath or shower, bring scented candles, let this time bring tenderness to your soul and if you want, to play soft music or instrumental music so the steam and this music rest you... Enjoy your life, live with God and rejoice because God loves you.

God has made us in a way that joy and humor are vital parts of our lives. The connection between our emotional health and physical health is undeniable. Those with a joyful and positive outlook are far more likely to have better physical health. It's not a guarantee that the joyful will never get sick, but their ability to recover and cope with illness is greatly enhanced. Conversely, those who rarely laugh or spend long periods in overly serious states have less of an ability to handle the stress of illness and disease. Those with long-term depression–what the Bible calls "a broken spirit"–often have physically declining health that parallels their emotional illness.

Laugh regularly and keep a positive and cheerful spirit, it will be a blessing for your body. Keep your body well-nourished so it is a blessing for your emotions.

Seventh Meditation

Forgiveness is a critical part of navigating relationships and taking care of your heart with compassion. For Jesus, forgiveness is of paramount importance. It is the flip side of the love coin. Jesus wants us to love one another as he has loved us, and he explained that how people will know that we are his disciples is by the love we have for one another, "love one another as I have love you" (John 15:12).

It doesn't come easy and forgiveness is a fierce practice. So often, we damage our relationship with God and others when we sin. We must face what is difficult, to step into a swamp of deep sorrow and even grief at the time. Forgiveness is the way to turn the coin back to heads and return to love.

Jesus often spoke about forgiveness, forgave those who sinned against others, forgave those who sinned against him, and asked the Church to continue his healing ministry. Jesus taught, "If you forgive others their transgressions, your heavenly Father will forgive you" (Matthew 6:14). Peter asked Jesus how often it is necessary to forgive, and Jesus replied, "Seventy-seven times" (Matthew t 18:22), a number to be taken symbolically, not literally, for the never-ending way we ought to forgive.

Forgiveness starts with acceptance. By acknowledging the truth of a situation, you activate a higher level of thinking and widen your perspective. That doesn't mean you should condone harmful behavior but taking a minute to separate biases from reality can give you the space to respond with courage, intelligence, and compassion. Acceptance connects you with your deepest, wisest loving self, even in the face of strong emotions. Physical therapy taught me this, it can take repeated practice and time, and as I shared previously, *sometimes I felt that I will never recover.* Jesus was extremely kind and merciful to me as I recovered and He is kind and merciful to you too.

After the resurrection, Jesus breathed on the disciples and said, "Receive the Holy Spirit. Whose sins you forgive are forgiven them" (John 20:22-23). The more you see that others are similar to you, the more empathy you can feel. I invite you to consider these three practices:

- **Acknowledge and accept the hurt.** Don't be afraid to feel you are hurting. Maybe you have been betrayed. It's ok to feel disappointed and even to grieve. Turn to Jesus and Mary and ask them to accompany you.
- **Be open.** Be careful not to judge. Understand what happened, examine the situation. There is no right or wrong answer. Whatever the situation was, there are two parts of the story.
- **Forgive yourself.** Caress yourself with a gentle touch on your arm and heart to calm your body.

Holy Mary, Mother of God

We live in a world full of noise. Our technologies and our way of life make it difficult for us to set aside time and space to be calm and reflect. More often, we should be alone with our thoughts and thus "go into ourselves".

What would help? The answer is the prayer of the **ROSARY**. Mary will teach us to grow in our relationship with God, and thus enter into ourselves... to value silence and solitude. For my family, praying the rosary has become a part of our lives. We need to be clear there will never be a better time than now to wholeheartedly respond to the call to holiness. Who knows how much longer we will be alive on this earth?

The Rosary helped us value silence and allows us to open our hearts to God. If we recite the rosary with mercy, with love for Jesus and Mary, it will lead us to the presence of God. Let us remember that the rosary was the prayer of the saints, it was the secret of their holiness, the rosary is the direct cause of their closeness to Christ. It was even the only prayer prayed for many years after the Mother of God (Mary) revealed it to Santo Domingo de Guzmán in an apparition in the year 1208. The recitation of the rosary was the most prayed prayer for almost two centuries. But it was in the Battle of Lepanto, where because of this battle that the prayer of the rosary took on a lot of boom and popularity. The Muslims controlled the Mediterranean Sea and were preparing to invade Europe. The Catholic kings of Europe were divided and did not realize the imminent danger. Pope Pius V (1566 - 1572) asked for help, but he was not paid much attention until the danger became very palpable and the invasion was certain. On September 17, 1569, he asked that the Holy Rosary be prayed. Finally, the two fleets met on October 7, 1571, the Christian and the Muslim had a confrontation in the Gulf of Corinth, near the Greek city of Lepanto. The Christian fleet, made up of soldiers from the Papal States, Venice, Genoa, and Spain, went into battle. Before the attack, the Christian troops prayed the Holy Rosary with great devotion. The battle of Lepanto lasted until late in the afternoon, but the Christians were victorious, preventing the invasion of Europe by Muslim troops.

In the book "Breath: The New Science of a Last Art" written by James Nestor, I was highly surprised because I never imagined that praying the rosary would help so much. I share what impressed me from this reading:

In 2001, researchers at the University of Pavia in Italy gathered up a dozen people, covered them with sensors to measure blood flow, heart rate and the nervous system, and then asked them to pray the rosary, the Catholic prayer of the Ave Maria. They were surprised to discover that the average number of breaths for each cycle was "exactly" identical.

But what was even more surprising was what happened when they breathed. Each time they followed this slow breathing pattern, blood flow to the brain increased and the body system entered a state of coherence. The heart, body circulation and nervous system were coordinated to achieve maximum efficiency.

But the most efficient breathing rate occurred when both the breath duration and the total breaths were in amazingly coordinated symmetry: 5.5-second inhalations followed by 5.5-second exhalations, which equates to almost exactly 5.5 breaths per minute.

We believe that the rosary is in sync with inherent cardiovascular rhythms and therefore gives a sense of well-being and perhaps a greater responsiveness to the religious message. The meditations, Hail Mary's, and dozens of other prayers developed over the past thousands of years are not without foundation.[1]

Jesus wants to be born in each one of us. He wants his life to become ours, and our lives to become his. The rosary could be that prayer that leads us to this transformation, apart as James Nestor says, this will help us with the benefits that coordinating breathing brings us.

Next, I share with you a letter that Rocío Chávez, wife of my nephew Javier, wrote me. The letter expresses the feeling of my family during the time I was in the hospital and how the family became closer through the Rosary. This letter came when I was in Marysville and it was one more

---

1   Nestor, James. *Breath: The New Science of a Lost Art. Riverhead Books, New York.* 2020.

motivation that helped me to continue fighting during my convalescence, I remember that I was sitting on the bed in the room assigned to me and I don't know what I was thinking at that moment, but suddenly one nurse came in exclaiming --- *Wow! You have a lot of mail---*. She had my mail in her hand, with the letter that had come from California, I opened the letter and read it without knowing it would bring a wealth of emotions that brought me to tears, in reading this letter, I knew and I understood many things; among others, how much my family had suffered for me and my illness. As well as the many times they left everything behind to come together in prayer and ask for me during the rosaries.

Next, I want to share with you the content of the letter:

We are happy to see him so recovered. That God granted us the miracle of having him among us is something for which we will always be grateful. The pandemic has affected many families and we never imagined what the Saldívar Family would go through. We clearly remember the rosary that you began to ask God Our Lord for his protection during the pandemic.

The first days when we came together through zoom, we did not imagine the path we would travel united in prayer. It is as if from the beginning God not only began to work in you but in the whole family. It was as if through the union of the rosary, you were preparing your family for a difficult task, where there were moments of great sadness and where sometimes faith approved. Although it was difficult, from the beginning God was with all of us. Witnessing through zoom how his medical situation was getting worse was not easy, but without realizing it, it was the beginning of a familiar process that God already had for us. The more days passed the more family members united in prayer.

The time of the rosary was the time when we anxiously wanted to know how your health was. Your niece, Adriana, had a huge responsibility being in charge of zoom as were Natalie and Father Juan José, who were the ones in charge of informing us about your medical condition. COVID-19 is a virus that is still unknown. Because of this, on many occasions the doctors did not have the answers to our questions. As you already know, in your family there are always different opinions and perspectives, sometimes emotions run high. The sensitivity was felt through the screen, all of us in our own way were worried, nervous, sad and very affected by your state of health.

One of the moments where many hearts broke was when we saw you intubated and depending on other devices that worked to mount you and keep you alive. The cry of pain, that was heard through the screen, was hard braking for us. However, the faith, the rosaries and the chains of prayer, kept us on our feet and with great hope, especially seeing that day by day you became stronger and stronger. We wondered why Father Roberto was in this situation. Why were you the one who got sick this way? The more we wondered why you, the clearer it became to me that God had a very special purpose for the whole family and especially in your life. Your recovery was a miracle. I concluded that you are an uncle, brother, and a much loved and respected human being.

Javier and I talked about how special you are for all of us and how in one way or another, you have touched our hearts. That is why with FAITH we are here asking God to heal you. In those moments where the love, that the family has for you, was expressed it is that I understood why you, Father Roberto, are the one to unite our family more. All of us who lived through this process with you were touched by God in an impressive way.

During those difficult times, we remembered that you have always been there for us when we needed it most, and now once again you joined us in prayer. Javier and I remember, and are infinitely grateful, that you listened to us when we most needed advice fact of listening to us and guiding us with your wisdom, we will always thank you for listening. During the time of your hospitalization, at times when the doctors did not give the family encouraging news, Javier was devastated. He had never been so sad except when his Mama Chole died.

September 23 was one of the most difficult moments for us. It was that afternoon when they urgently had to transfer you from one hospital to another. It was one of the days that we were uncertain. What will happened in the transfer? You had us in great anguish. That was the day that many left everything and joined the rosary to pray for you; prayer was the link that kept us together as a family. You were the most important thing; you were the priority. That day there were those who joined the rosary for the first time. The spirit of God was present, as we prayed with all the faith in our hearts. I remember that Juan Enrique (your sister Alicia's son) suggested that we pray another rosary during his transfer.

It was a day full of uncertainty, the doctors changed the plan of his transfer and in the they took him by helicopter, since his condition was critical as was the weather. Luckily, he didn't notice the transfer, despite the storm. He was in the ICU for a long time and on ECMO, as his lungs were failing by then. In fact, his entire system was failing. The medical staff told us that there was little hope that he would survive and the decision had to be made to keep him alive by machines. We continue in prayer.

For Javier and me, it was difficult to realize the seriousness of his state of health because precisely on September 24 we celebrated 15 years of marriage. With hearts full of emotions, we remembered the day you married us, and now on this important date you were between life and death. That reality hurt us a lot. You didn't know it, but days before you got sick, we were saying that we wanted you to give us your blessing via zoom on our anniversary. Seeing how the virus affected you more and more, we realized that it would not be possible. The moment came, when with tears in his eyes, Javier told me that the only thing he wanted for our anniversary was for you to be well. With great faith we asked God for your recovery. On September 24, we were pleased that you were transferred to the new hospital, at Providence. In fact, God allowed us to go to the Mary Magdalene Church in Camarillo, where you married us. We wanted to thank God for giving us hope that you would be okay. Our faith was strengthened and, although in the following days the doctors gave us little hope, we remained strong.

Father Roberto, you touched our lives in a special way. When we visited you in Portland, Oregon, it was very difficult to see you in the hospital with many machines attached to your body. Knowing you were there, but not having communication with you was painful; however, being able to be there strengthened Javier's faith.

In one of the times that he was with you, when making eye contact, he felt that you heard him while he was talking to you. In his heart he knew that you would recover. Seeing you on zoom, and excited and full of hope for your book, gives us great joy. You are a beautiful miracle that God gave us. In fact, you joined people of all faiths in praying for your recovery. Praying was not a matter of religion but of faith to ask for your healing. Thank you for everything you continue to teach us and share. It is beautiful to receive your blessing.

As a thank you to my family and the people who joined the rosary via Zoom to pray for my recovery, I want to offer this Hail Mary.

Hail Mary,
Full of Grace,
The Lord is with thee.
Blessed art thou among women,
and blessed is the fruit
of thy womb, Jesus.

Holy Mary,
Mother of God,
pray for us sinners now,
and at the hour of our death.
Amen.

God Loves us Healthy

I never thought to explore the bible to verify that God wants us to be healthy... I have preached how God heals us, but not how he heals us. I have shared retreats where I have prayed to God for healing. I had never had to develop this idea that **'God wants us healthy,'** biblically. We can never monopolize or exhaust a subject as extensive as the subject of health. But it was a good exercise for me, finding 50 biblical texts that refer to the fact that God wants us to be healthy.[1] I do not even mention the book of Tobias where, through the archangel Raphael Tobias, makes a balm with the entrails of a fish, to help heal the blindness of Tobit, his father.

The New Testament names only two archangels, Michael and Gabriel (Luke 1: 9–26; Jude 1:9; Revelation 12:7), but it is believed that the archangel Raphael is also referred to in the Gospel of John (5:2–4),[2] where Jesus heals a paralytic in the pool of "Bethesda". I was baptized in the Church of Saint Raphael and my mother always invited to invoke him in

---

1   *There are many more biblical quotes that show that God wants to heal us, in fact, the Bible as a whole is that.*

2   *An angel of the Lord used to come down into the pool; and the water was stirred up, so the first one to get in, after the stirring of the water, was healed of whatever disease afflicted him.*

any need I might have. The name Raphael means "healing of God", so he is the patron saint of doctors, sick people and hospitals. The Church links Raphael with Michael and Gabriel as saints whose intercession can be sought through prayer.

It is unfortunate and it is also a mistake to attribute suffering to God saying it is his will. NO, God wants the best for us, we should never doubt it. For this reason and as a conclusion, I have included these biblical quotes, confirming that God wants us to be healthy. God wants to heal us, the reason Jesus died on the Cross was to save us and to heal us. Always remember it, don't forget it.

These biblical quotes were a great blessing; It is a useful material to study later. I want to be clear that I am only talking about health, many times when we talk about health we think of wounds. God wants us to have life, to have life in abundance. Christ himself says: "I have come so that they may have life, and have more abundantly (John 10, 10)."

I hope that with these biblical texts, you can discover that life in abundance can be lived in the same illness, although it seems contradictory. A sick person can be healthy, although this again seems ironic.

Think about your body: do you know that it is always battling all type of germs? Everything around us is teeming with microbes. We are always in battle. God has made the human body so wonderful, that while we go from here to there our body is constantly working against viruses... hence the importance of taking vitamins, our mother would say. As I explained earlier, God has given us an incredible immune system to defend ourselves against whatever may attack the body. Now as you read what I write your body is breathing and processing the oxygen entering through your nose and is eliminating toxins, carbon dioxide, other types of negative substances, while your blood is running through your veins.

Your cells, which are like little health factories, are collecting the toxins and waste that your body is generating. White cells are fighting infections, if you were infected, they are fighting to keep you healthy. Now think about your nose, it is filtering out pollen and dust, plus a number of other things you are not even realizing, all the time it is filtering out strange things from the air you breathe, and if you smell bad, it warns you to notice and cover your nose. Our nose in these last two years has been happy that we use *'mouth covers'*, it would say: *'finally you realize the importance of protecting myself, thank you.'* Isn't our body a wonder?

'God wants us to be healthy' But there is also a lot of evil around us, think about the things that harm us in this world, things that do not come from God... now think about the things that do not come from God, but by choice you want them or seek them, even knowing they harm you. We are constantly tempted, right? We decide if we fall or not. If we are physically and spiritually healthy then we can resist. Remember that your body is well equipped and if it is not, due to any situation or illness you are suffering, you have the Holy Spirit of God within you that will lead you towards the truth, with Him you can move forward: perfecting and sanctifying yourself.

'God wants us to be healthy.' In Romans 8:28, it says: "We know that all things work for good for those who love God, who are called according to his purpose." This verse from Saint Paul to the Romans does not imply that we will not suffer, Jesus himself told us "...in the world you will have trouble, but take courage, I have conquered the world" (John 16, 33). Let us say to the Lord: 'Father, renew my perspective so that I can understand my health in difficult times of illness and struggle, with my imperfections of character, when I fall into temptation or practices that You have not blessed. Allow me to emerge victorious from any situation that is not pleasant for you.

'God wants us to be healthy.' If you are going through difficulties if you are going through a time of spiritual drought, of illness, of struggle. If you are struggling with something in your life, entrust yourself to the Lord, abandoning yourself to Him, rest in Him and do not stop doing good while you are struggling, keep trusting. Christ has come into the world so we may have life in abundance. He has died on the cross, He shed His blood, He shed His life for us, His body was wounded, for our sins so that the evil that wants to rule this world and reign over us is annihilated. When we celebrate the Eucharist and remember the body and blood of Christ shed for us, at that moment let us remember that in that crucifixion of the Lord there is life, there is power, there is triumph over all circumstances.

'God wants us to be healthy.' Jesus' mission began with healings. He responded to people's aches and pains. It was a first and modest sign he came as a bringer of life to alleviate many afflictions. Christianity is a physical religion. The 'spiritual life' is better understood in terms of bodily activity, breathing, hearing, seeing, touching, walking, eating and drinking, the Lord touches and sanctifies each action so they are lived to the full, thus opening himself to the transcendent. All our senses are sanctified. May these 50 biblical quotes help you to delve into it...

145

Old Testament

1) He said: If you listen closely to the voice of the LORD, your God, and do what is right in his eyes: if you heed his commandments and keep all his statutes, I will not afflict you with any of the diseases with which I afflicted the Egyptians; for I, the LORD, am your healer (Exodus 15:26).

2) You shall serve the LORD, your God; then he will bless your food and drink, and I will remove sickness from your midst (Exodus 23: 25).

3) The LORD will remove all sickness from you; he will not afflict you with any of the malignant diseases (Deuteronomy 7:15).

4) May the LORD give might to his people; may the LORD bless his people with peace! (Psalm 29:11).

5) I will pardon all your sins, and heal all your ills (Psalm 103:3).

6) Sent forth his word to heal them (Psalm 107:20).

7) This will mean health for your flesh and vigor for your bones (Proverbs 3:8).

8) For they are life to those who find them, bringing health to one's whole being (Proverbs 4:22).

9) A joyful heart is the health of the body, but a depressed spirit dries up the bones (Proverbs 17:22).

10) The eyes of those who see will not be closed; the ears of those who hear will be attentive (Isaiah 32:3).

11) Then the lame shall leap like a stag, and the mute tongue sing for joy (Isaiah 35:6).

12) Yours is the life of my spirit. You have given me health and restored my life! (Isaiah 38:16).

13) He gives power to the faint, abundant strength to the weak (Isaiah

40:29).

14) They will soar on eagles' wings; they will run and not grow weary, walk and not grow faint (Isaiah 40:31).

15) Even to your old age I am he, even when your hair is gray, I will carry you; I have done this, and I will lift you up, I will carry you to safety (Isaiah 46:4).

16) Peace to those who are far and near, says the LORD; and I will heal them (Isaiah 57:19).

17) Your wound shall quickly be healed (Isaiah 58:8).

18) For I will restore your health; I will heal your injuries—oracle of the LORD (Jeremiah 30:17).

19) Behold I will bring it health and cure, and I will cure you, and will reveal unto you the abundance of peace and truth (Jeremiah 33:6).

20) Listen! I will make breath enter you so you may come to life (Ezekiel 37:5).

New Testament

21) I will come and cure him (Matthew 8:17).

22) Those who are well do not need a physician, but the sick do (Matthew 9:12).

23) His heart was moved with pity for them, and he cured the sick (Matthew 14:14).

24) Jesus went about curing every disease and illness among the people (Matthew 4:23).

25) Let it be done for you according to your faith (Matthew 9:29).

26) He summoned his twelve disciples and gave them authority over

unclean spirits to drive them out and to cure every disease and every illness (Matthew 10:1).

27) Many [people] followed him, and he cured them all (Matthew 12:15).

28) Begged him that they might touch only the tassel on his cloak, and as many as touched it were healed (Matthew 14:36).

29) He has done all things well. He makes the deaf hear and [the] mute speak (Mark 7:37).

30) They will lay hands on the sick, and they will recover (Mark 16:18)

31) Jesus rebuked the unclean spirit, healed the boy, and returned him to his father (Luke 9:42).

32) Jesus spoke to them about the kingdom of God, and he healed those who needed to be cured (Luke 9:11).

33) I am the resurrection and the life; whoever believes in me, even if he dies, will live, and everyone who lives and believes in me will never die (Juan 11:25-26)

34) And by faith in his name, this man, whom you see and know, his name has made strong, and the faith that comes through it has given him this perfect health, in the presence of all of you (Acts 3:16).

35) Stretch forth [your] hand to heal (Acts 4:30).

36) "Get up and make your bed." He got up at once (Acts 9:34).

37) He went about doing good and healing (Acts 10:38).

38) When face clothes were touched his skin and applied to the sick, their diseases left them (Acts 19:12).

39) If the Spirit of the one who raised Jesus from the dead dwells in you, the one who raised Christ from the dead will give life (Romans 8:11).

40) He rescued us from such great danger of death, and he will continue to rescue us; in him we have put our hope [that] he will also rescue us again (2 Corinthians 1:10).

41) To another gifts of healing by the one Spirit (1 Corinthians 12:9).

42) That it may go well with you and that you may have a long life on earth (Ephesians 6:3).

43) He delivered us from the power of darkness and transferred us to the kingdom of his beloved Son (Colossians 1:13).

44) The Lord will rescue me from every evil threat and will bring me safe to his heavenly kingdom (2 Timothy 4:18).

45) Our bodies washed in pure water (Hebrews 10:10).

46) Strengthen your drooping hands and your weak knees. Make straight paths for your feet, that what is lame may not be dislocated but healed (Hebrews 12:12-13).

47) Is anyone among you sick? He should summon the presbyters of the church, and they should pray over him and anoint [him] with oil in the name of the Lord, and the prayer of faith will save the sick person, and the Lord will raise him up. If he has committed any sins, he will be forgiven (James 5:14-15).

48) Therefore, confess your sins to one another and pray for one another, that you may be healed. The fervent prayer of a righteous person is very powerful (James 5:16).

49) He himself bore our sins in his body upon the cross, so that, free from sin, we might live for righteousness. By his wounds you have been healed (1 Peter 2:24).

50) Let the one who thirsts come forward, and the one who wants it

receive the gift of life-giving water (Revelation 22:17).

Conclusion

This pandemic (COVID-19) has transformed the world and even though our immune system is our body's natural defense, given by God to protect us against external agents that can cause us harm (toxins, bacteria, viruses, poisons, etc.), the Coronavirus weakened our immune system. Many of us got sick and became weak, and we infected others unintentionally. So, the chances of getting sick increased without our knowing how.

Now the million-dollar question is, how long will we be like this? I think it's a hard question to answer because many factors complicate a correct answer. But the important thing is this experience has led us to recognize that we need each other. The pandemic has made us awaken to the reality of love which leads us to understand God more fully.

To live in the clarity of God is to be freed from fear and death; our existence will not end in emptiness. It will reach the fullness of life. That is why the invitation not to be afraid has its strength in the love of Christ Jesus our Lord who gives us the strength to live life at the right time.

Death itself, experienced from this divine viewpoint, is not an evil to be feared as the worst thing that can happen. Human life will not end in a vacuum; one day we humans will calmly arrive into the loving arms of God. The invitation not to be afraid has its strength and foundation in the love of Christ Jesus capable of giving us what we most need so our joy may be full.

We must not fear any pandemic. Love must be the school of preparation for those who believe. If you have never experienced love, it will be difficult for you to be happy. Love equals "salvation" which is achieved more easily when we accept our imperfections.

This pandemic helped me to go deeper and become more aware of my shortcomings. It sharpened my senses (sight, smell, taste, and touch), which make me feel more alive. I am more sensitive; I can be easily hurt. COVID softened my emotions and nourished me more than I thought, which is why my heart hurts much more easily when it gets hurt. The poet and painter William Blake (1757-1827) understood my feeling well and describes it in this poem:

> *Mercy has a human heart,*
> *Pity a human face,*
> *And Love, the human form divine,*
> *And Peace, the human dress.*[1]

I hope that reading this book helped you to be more sensitive, you lose nothing, on the contrary, you could gain a lot. Life is a constant change and improves when we accept suffering and pain accepted and offered to God with joy.

My healing gladdened my heart, I have lived again, but now with a

---

1   William Blake, 'The Divine Image', *Complete Works*, p. 117.

new purpose, a mission. The miracle has opened me to love. God invites me to find the essential of life, its mystery that transforms the heart in gratitude.

There is a song by the Argentine duet "Pimpinela" called, '*The year that time stopped*', I think this song sums up the feelings of many people. When you have time, I invite you to listen to it:

I have felt a sadness I never felt
I've missed even the people I didn't know
I've seen how life goes in a moment

The year that time stood still
I have cried like I never ever cried
I've prayed for what I never prayed for
I've struggled with heartache and thoughts

The year that time stood still
And although everything will pass and although we will continue
Something has changed, something has helped
And although everything will pass, this has to unite us
For those who are no longer with us, and we couldn't say goodbye.
I've felt all the fear I ever felt
I have suffered the bitterness of what I lost
I have carried the impotence of what I do not understand
The year that time stood still
And although everything will pass, and although we will continue

Something has to change, something has to help
And although everything will pass, this has to unite us
For those who are no longer with us and we couldn't say goodbye.

It is up to us to keep hope alive. We advance when we love each other, we will advance when we love each other; we will move forward when we are inclusive. Live love despite the losses you have experienced: the death of loved ones, pain and isolated suffering. Against all odds.

In Gratitude

Wnat is the effect of a book on the reader? How do you measure its scope, meaning, depth, and wisdom? Writing a book is always complex. Writing is like a spiritual collaboration between the writer and you, the reader. I hope and pray that what I wrote will reach your sensitivity.

Help me to thank God for the miracle of life. I am personally grateful, and I will always be grateful to my community, the Missionaries of the Holy Spirit of the Christ the Priest Province, and especially to my family who supported me throughout this entire process. A special thanks to Fr. Mario Rodríguez, M.Sp.S., for reading the first draft and inviting me to make corrections and for helping me with the grammar. Your perspective, Mario, was very helpful. Thank you for your friendship and for being there for me when I was hospitalized.

I am grateful to Most Rev. Gustavo García-Siller, M.Sp.S., Archbishop of San Antonio, Texas for reading the first draft and writing the foreword. I also want to thank Carmen Morga for writing the introduction, Carmen accompanied me psychologically and helped me to transition back to life easier. Thanks to Joan Kluck, who helped me with the English translation; and to Alexandro (Chuchin) Azpeitia, who helped me edit this book and with my Spanish. The two gave me feedback when talking to them about the chapters. Your insights and ideas were very helpful and meaningful to me, thank you.

I am blessed to have a beautiful niece, Natalie Saldívar, who collaborated with me by writing her experience. She, along with every member of my family, suffered when they found out that I had COVID. I also thank Rocío, wife of my nephew Javier Chávez, who collaborated by sharing the theme "Holy Mary, Mother of God". This was a letter she sent while I was convalescing in Marysville and in which she shares the experience she, her husband and the family had as they gathered to pray the rosary. What the doctors shared did not help her believe in miracles, but her faith remained strong as she prayed the rosary. Thank you, Natalie, and Rocío for sharing your faith with my readers.

Finally, I thank Manuel Loyola for the cover; you definitely did a beautiful design, I am very impressed by your work and your talent. Thank you, Manuel, for your friendship.

In this book, you have read several poems and songs, you may wonder why. During this recovery time, my mind was nourished by them. They were a gift from God to me; music, poetry and silence helped me in this difficult time to find peace. Let me share one last short poem from Rabindranath Tagore:[1]

---

1   *Rabindranath Tagore (1861-1941) is from India and won the Nobel Prize of Literature in 1913. With his poems he has become famous in the West. In fact, his fame attained a luminous height, taking him across continents on lecture.*

I slept and dreamed that life was joy.
I wake up and see that the life was service.
I acted and behold; the service was joy.

I want to thank and honor the many doctors and nurses at St. Vincent Medical Hospital, Providence Medical Center, and Marysville Rehab Center who, though they believed I would surely die, took extraordinary care of me. In the book of Sirach 38: 1-10 God himself invites us to be grateful to the doctors for the knowledge he gives them for our care:

Make friends with the doctor, for he is essential to you;
God has also established him in his profession.
From God the doctor has wisdom,
and from the king he receives sustenance.
Knowledge makes the doctor distinguished,
and gives access to those in authority.
God makes the earth yield healing herbs
which the prudent should not neglect;
Was not the water sweetened by a twig,
so that all might learn his power?
He endows people with knowledge,
to glory in his mighty works,
Through which the doctor eases pain,
and the druggist prepares his medicines.
Thus, God's work continues without cease
in its efficacy on the surface of the earth.

My son, when you are ill, do not delay,
but pray to God, for it is he who heals.
Flee wickedness and purify your hands;
cleanse your heart of every sin.

For their attention I thank my family and brother priests. Thanks to each of you for taking the time to read this book. Crossing the threshold of dead, I live.

Thank you
Roberto Saldívar-Ureño, M.Sp.S.

Dedication

The pandemic changed the lifestyle of many people, undoubtedly some things will never be the same as before. Even with all the restrictions that have been taken, COVID continues to transform our lives in many ways, and it also continues to uproot lives.

These losses have caused tremendous pain and emptiness, and now fear and pain are preventing us from living life to the fullest. We would like to go through this pain, and come out strengthened in sensitivity, in essence, in knowledge and in the love for living. However, this is not what usually happens. As I look around me, I don't see this desired change; it will take our dependence on God to cause this outcome.

Within each one of us is this truth, saying goodbye to our loved ones makes their death affect us, but we must continue in this world living a life as normal as possible, this is achieved thanks to hope and love that the Holy Spirit gives us.

Is it easy? No, because suffering is real; it hurts. This is and will continue to be the feeling of my sister Alicia, who continues to suffer because of the death of her son Ricardo; she suffers his absence. I have also suffered because I who am his uncle and was godfather. The whole family has missed him; his absence is conspicuous. Although the years pass, we will always remember him.

I have dedicated my book to Ricardo because long time ago when I decided to write my story of the miracle that God did in me, I had a dream... I dreamed of Ricardo who was in front of a waterfall surrounded by trees. When I saw him, I asked him, 'What are you doing?' --- 'I'm looking at the waterfall', he replied respectfully as usual; I couldn't contain my laughter, because it was obvious that he wasn't seeing it, because he had his back to it and the water from the waterfall soaked his clothes. --- 'godfather I don't have to be in front to see the waterfall, I look at it with the eyes of my soul', was his answer, this surprised me for sounding so illogical. When I woke up, I wanted to interpret the dream, but it was later that I understood... 'seeing with the soul' is seeing the emotions and accepting them unconditionally. Without labels, without past or future. My nephew now sees freely, without attachments and without fear. He loves in a perfect and pure way, just as in the waterfall he is drenched, but now he is drenched in love, also now like the water, he is transparent.

Ricardo was an efficient, talented and honest young man. He hoped to be a policeman, and he admired his cousin Jesús Chávez who is a policeman. He shared many moments with his cousin whom he admired and respected greatly... Jesus is also my nephew. My mom was very fond of him, she was so proud of him and when he came home dressed in his uniform... I told her I was jealous because she used to take pictures with him and not with me -- I told her that to make her smile.

Ricardo was also proud of his cousin Jesus, they used to have fun whenever the opportunity arose. Jesus suggested that he enter the academy --- and that is how he participated in the academy and attended all the required courses and camps. His first formal job, which would help him achieve his goal, was to patrol the streets of the city and break badly parked cars. It was a simple and fun job for him, but not for those who were fined, because when they returned, they found the ticket with the fine in the car.

Ricardo was attentive to his family, he was "kind" growing up, and he liked to study. He was respectful with his parents, and he especially loved his sister Adriana since the two were close in age...

Before he died, I had the opportunity to hear his confession and give him the anointing of the sick, I also celebrated mass in his room. When I said goodbye, I told him that when he gets to heaven, to greet the Blessed Virgin Mary on my behalf and to ask Conchita why she did not intercede for him to heal from cancer --- 'Yes, I will greet the Virgin Mary and Conchita, but I will not I'll tell Conchita that,' and he smiled at me with that answer. The last words I heard from him were, 'godfather, I'm leaving happy, God wanted it this way, everything is fine.' Before leaving his room, I approached him and kissed his forehead, offering one last blessing. I returned to Portland and during the flight and I wept silently on the plane remembering his words: 'Everything is fine.' The last time I saw him was during my convalescence when I had to celebrate Mass for his funeral.

I never thought I would celebrate another funeral after my mother's funeral, much less in such adverse conditions due to my deplorable health. My family was happy to see me now alive celebrating mass, but it was difficult for them to accept that I was celebrating mass for my nephew, they would rather have wanted it to be a thanksgiving mass for my recovery.

Everything that is not resolved in the heart will try to find answers,

161

my nephew Ricardo knew that he would die and told his mother not to question God with questions about why he did not heal him. When our loved ones die, we will have answers of 'Why?' They will not be given to us because we could not understand them. It is about living death and feeling that pain in the heart giving thanks for life.

Grief is that experience of pain, pity, affliction or resentment that manifests itself in different ways when we lose someone or something significant to us. Life is change and changes are always accompanied by losses. You can't not feel pain or pretend it doesn't hurt to lose the one you love. But in death there is also room to smile and rejoice.

I remember reading something that is attributed to the famous Leonardo da Vinci,

Just like a day well spent
produces a sweet dream,
so, a life well spent
causes a sweet death.

My nephew Ricardo had a sweet death because he had a beautiful life. The popular saying that we often hear (common in in Spanish) --- 'nobody knows what was lost until it is no longer there' --- does not apply to Ricardo.

I invite you to reflect on a thought of Socrates: "The fear of death is nothing more than considering yourself wise without being so, since it is believing you know about what you do not know. Perhaps death is the greatest blessing of the human being, nobody knows it, and yet everyone fears it as if they knew with absolute certainty that it is the worst of evils." Death rips us out of physical life but if we are not ripped out, we can choose to live thinking that death is a blessing. With this we have nothing to lose. Dorothy Day lived it as an experience of pruning, in this experience she understood the biblical text of John 15: 1-8 and reflects:

> *The only answer to the mystery of suffering is this: every soul seeks happiness either in creatures or in God. God made us for himself. We must die to the natural to achieve the supernatural, a slow death or a quick one. It is universal. Unless the grain of wheat fall into the ground and die, it remains alone, but if it dies, it bears much fruit. All must die; it is a universal law very hard for us to realize.*
>
> *If this mind or this flesh is an obstacle, we will suffer the more when this tremendous lover tries to tear from us all veils which separate us. Some suffering is more visible, some hidden. The more we long for love, the more all human love will be pruned.... It is a pruning, a cutting away of love so that it will grow strong and bear much fruit....*

Death is a real event... it will come. We may be invaded by the feeling it is not true that he has died. It's a real stage of denial that we saw. That is why we must come to acceptance. The first days and weeks after Ricardo's death, my sister Alicia was still in a state of shock, unable to recognize the magnitude of her pain. One of my brothers insisted that she accept it, Ricardo is dead, it is a reality. But she replies, 'you don't know the pain one feels because you haven't lost a child' and she was right.

Many times, we want to help someone who has suffered the death of a loved one, but we must avoid these comments: 'you shouldn't feel like this', 'don't cry anymore', 'cheer up, everything will pass, everything will be fine'. We must allow those who suffer the death of a loved one to express their grief, anger, feelings and thoughts of pain, which overwhelm them. Cry, scream, curse, or stare into infinity. We could better give a hug, a hug without scolding, let the suffering express itself.

I want to share a poem by the Uruguayan writer and poet Mario Benedetti, "No Te Rindas" (Don't Give up). If you have lost a loved one due to the pandemic or illness, such was the case of my sister, I invite you to meditate slowly:

Don't give up, you still have time
to reach up and start anew,
Accept your shadows,
Bury your fears,
Free your burdens,
Fly again.

Don't give up, that's what life is
Continue the journey,
Follow your dreams,
Unstuck time,
Move the rubble,
And uncover the sky.

Don't give up, please don't give way,
Even if the cold burns,
Even if fear bites,
Even if the sun sets,
And the wind goes silent,
There is still fire in your soul
There is still life in your dreams.

Because life is yours and yours is the desire
Because you have loved it and because I love you
Because wine exists and love is true.
Because there are no wounds that time doesn't cure.
To open the doors,
Take away the locks,

Abandon the walls that have protected you,
To live life and accept the challenge
Get back laughter,
Practice a song,
Lower the guard and extend the hands
Open the wings
And try again,
Celebrate life and take back the skies,

Don't give up, please don't give way,
Even if the cold burns,

Even if fear bites,
Even if the sun sets,
And the wind goes silent,
There is still fire in your soul
There is still life in your dreams.
Because every day is a new beginning,
Because this is the hour and the best moment.
Because you are not alone, because I love you.